Original
JOHN DEERE
Letter Series Tractors
1923–1954

Brian Rukes and Andy Kraushaar

MBI Publishing Company

First published in 2001 by MBI Publishing Company, Galtier Plaza, Suite 200, 380 Jackson Street, St. Paul, MN 55101-3885 USA

MBI Publishing Company books are also available at discounts in bulk quantity for industrial or sales-promotional use. For details write to Special Sales Manager at Motorbooks International Wholesalers & Distributors, Galtier Plaza, Suite 200, 380 Jackson Street, St. Paul, MN 55101-3885 USA.

Edited by Darwin Holmstrom
Designed by LeAnn Kuhlmann

Printed in Hong Kong

Library of Congress Cataloging-in-Publication Data
Rukes, Brian.
    Original John Deere letter series tractors: 1923–1954 / Brian Rukes & Andy Kraushaar.
        p. cm.
    Includes index.
    ISBN 0-7603-0912-4 (hc. : alk. paper)
        1. John Deere tractors—History.
        I. Kraushaar, Andy.
TL233.6.J64 R8497 2001
629.225'2—dc21   2001030599

On the front cover: Like the BWH, the BWH-40s received styled lines. Note the differences in the markings on these tractors as well as the different positions of their air intake and exhaust stacks.

On the frontispiece: The strong grill treatment that Henry Dreyfuss applied to styled versions of John Deere's model A and B defined John Deere tractors for decades to come.

On the title page: Tipping the scales at around 7,400 pounds, Deere's Model R packed a powerful punch at both the belt and the drawbar. In conditions where the R didn't have enough weight, wheel weights usually made up the difference.

On the back cover: The late Model GP tractors featured what is commonly called a "square" engine; that is, the bore and stroke of the engine were the same: six inches. The Models HWH and HNH achieved the additional clearance under the rear axles by simply having larger rear wheels. Deere made huge 38-inch rear wheels standard equipment on the HWH and HNH.

Contents

Acknowledgments

I would like to extend an emphatic, heartfelt thank you to the people at Deere & Company Archives in Moline, Illinois, for allowing me access to the archives. The cooperation of the Deere Archives personnel, and that of Mr. Leslie Stegh in particular, was greatly appreciated. As always, it was a pleasure to work with those individuals. To each of you, thank you!!!

This book would also not have been possible were it not for the encouragement of many people. I would like to thank my father, Charles Rukes, for introducing me to these wonderful machines, and I would like to thank tractor collectors from around the world for their work in preserving this important part of our history. A special thanks goes out to Jim Cole and the members of the Oklahoma 2-Cylinder Club based in Fairview, Oklahoma, which hosts "The National" each year. My exposure to the two-cylinder John Deere tractors in that club and at that show has been invaluable to me in my current station.

The photographer wishes to thank the owners for the generous use of their time and tractors. Without the dedication of people like this, the magnificent tractors in this book would not exist: Herb Altenburg; Seno Bast; Richard Bockwoldt; John Caes; Robert Dufel; Del and Don Endres; Walter, Bruce, and Jason Keller; Don Kleven Jr.; Ken Koberg; Mike Kolb; Lester, Kenny, and Harland Layher; Howard and Bonnie Miller; Bob Olson; Bob and Mary Pollock; Myron Punzel; Bob Rettig; Jim Schmidt; Randy and Vernon Serstner; Derrick and Darold Sindt; Paul Steffes; Brian Steward; Ken Tank; Howard Ulrich; Herb Walter.

Introduction

Perhaps the best-known and most popular collectible tractors in the world are the letter-series John Deere two-cylinder tractors. These units have been the cornerstone of the tractor-collecting world for decades, and their popularity seems to always be on the rise. Indeed, within the last two decades tractor collecting as a whole has gained much popularity and has caught the attention of many.

Preserving our agricultural heritage is very important, for we don't want to forget where we've come from. These machines fed millions and helped employ multitudes of people. And these machines were a major part of the agricultural revolution—they helped replace animal power on farms with mechanical might. They made it possible to produce more food to feed more people, and all with less work. Today, agriculture can do so much more than it did then, but these tractors help set the gears of change in motion. These tractors—the John Deere letter-series tractors—helped make the technology of today a possibility.

There are many ways we can preserve these tractors, and any attempt to preserve them should be considered a noble one. If there is someone out there who wishes to preserve these tractors by participating with them in antique tractor pulls, so be it. If there is someone out there who wishes to farm with these tractors as they were designed to be used, that's great! And if there is someone out there who wants simply to "fix up" one of these machines to take to shows and parades, we should be glad. Purists might say that all of these tractors should be restored to immaculate condition, to the state in which they left the factory. Some would even like to be able to see their reflections in their paint jobs. To each his own. But no one should become so wrapped up or obsessed with "correct" restorations that they criticize others for how they are preserving these machines of the past. So, really, if someone decides to paint his or her John Deere lime green, that's his or her right. I'm not here to criticize anyone on how

they wish to "restore" their letter-series tractor, and I hope that you won't choose to criticize others in that regard either.

However, this book is supposed to give you some idea of what these John Deere letter-series tractors were originally like when they came into this world. And, to be quite honest, it would be impossible for anyone to say exactly how every single tractor looked when it rolled out of the factory. Odds are there was something different about each tractor, whether it be the features it had or the precise placement of its decals or the shade of its paint, even if those differences were so slight that they would be almost impossible to notice. But there are some guidelines that one can follow in a restoration, and this book attempts to outline some of those. Most of the references in this book are to the less-controversial topic of equipment; thus, this book attempts to outline when major mechanical changes took place, or when new variations of tractors appeared. This book also provides some information on generalized "rules" about the controversial topics of paint schemes and decal placement. Serial numbers are also a very important part of this book, as sometimes it is known at what serial number certain changes occurred or when certain things happened. This book does, indeed, go in depth, but due to the limited amount of space and words that could be included in it, the amount of information is also limited to some degree. However, the author has striven to include the information that he felt was the most important. All of this is an attempt to give you some idea of how you might try to preserve these wonderful machines.

The letter-series John Deere two-cylinder tractors have captured the minds and hearts of thousands of people from around the world. These machines catapulted Deere into the tractor industry, making the company a true full-line farm machinery company. Today, these tractors are remembered and admired by multitudes, and for good reason. These are their stories.

Chapter One

From Waterloo Boy to the John Deere D

For almost every major tractor manufacturer, there is a certain tractor that served as the cornerstone for the company, and every one of these tractors has a special story. For Deere & Company, that all-important tractor is the Model D. It was the tractor with the longest production run in company history, and, indeed, it is even the tractor with the longest-running production run of all tractors ever built, setting the record at an amazing 30 years. But to understand the D, you must understand what it was designed to do. So, let's take a journey.

Since we are dealing with Deere & Company, let's start our trek in Moline, Illinois, at the company's headquarters, and let's embark in June. To set out, let's jump right across the state line into Iowa, then drive west on Interstate 80. On our journey, we traverse over numerous large, beautiful hills, and along the way we witness a multitude of old barns and a number of old tractors sitting in the fencerows. Here, though, the majority of those tractors are of the row-crop design. Tractors of that design could operate well between planted rows, as found in corn and cotton fields, for instance. But the Model D wasn't that popular here; its standard-tread design limited its crop clearance. To understand the conditions in which the D was designed to be used, we must now drive further west.

I-80 eventually leads us into Omaha, Nebraska, a city that was once a branch house location for Deere. We continue driving, and before we get out of the hills of eastern Nebraska, we turn south onto Highway 81. This road, which slices right through the middle of the country, was perhaps the major north-south vein in the country before the advent of interstate highways. It was often used by harvesting crews as they worked their way up the Great Plains every summer. As we head south, we enter Kansas, where the land is so flat in places that you can see for miles, a characteristic typical of the Great Plains.

The Great Plains region of North America is vast, stretching from Texas all the way up through central Canada. Though the lay of the land changes drastically at times between those two places, most of the agricultural practices are the same from one end of the region to the other. Every year, thousands of farmers plant wheat in the late summer, hope

for nourishing rains in the months that follow, pray that hail and wind don't damage the crops, wait for the prairies to turn that beautiful golden color, and then start harvesting when the wheat is just right.

The further south we drive, the more the wheat has started to turn a golden color. By the time we arrive in northern Oklahoma, the wheat has bounteous heads of grain and is just right to harvest, and the harvest crews with their huge

combines are cutting their way across the rolling hills. Before we get very far south, we opt to exit highway 81 and head west. The land becomes more wide open and the winds pick up as we drive to the northwest corner of the state.

What is our final destination? It's Fairview, Oklahoma, and we arrive in mid-July. The temperatures are hot, peaking in the upper 90s and the low 100s, but the almost constant winds make the summers here bearable. But the temperatures don't matter to us, for we are about to attend one of the biggest working tractor expositions that exclusively features antique and classic John Deere products: "The National."

Opposite: Of all the letter-series John Deere tractors, the Model D had the longest production run. This venerable model has withstood the test of time and is still used actively in many locales.

The first tractor bearing the John Deere name, the Model D owed much to the Waterloo Boy tractors. The D featured many of the same characteristics of those tractors, including the horizontal two-cylinder engine.

Here, every year, they harvest wheat just as it was done in the old days. Here, you can take a journey back in time. And here you can always see a multitude of Model D John Deere tractors. Indeed, over 70 Ds were here for the 1993 show, which celebrated the D's 70th anniversary, and again, in 2000 (which was the 10th anniversary for this show), D attendance was also astounding.

And yes, here the Ds work just as they did starting in the mid-1920s. Each year at the show, Ds can be seen pulling binders, powering the threshing machines to separate the grain from the straw, powering the stationary hay presses to bale the straw, and then plowing under the fields of wheat stubble. The Ds here also do other things, including pulling large John Deere pull-type combines, which represent farming at a slightly later date or on a slightly larger scale. The D was a rugged machine, and it had to be.

as the Waterloo Boy Light Tractors, both the L and LA had opposed two-cylinder engines.

In the 1914 model year, the Waterloo Boy Model R came along to replace the Waterloo Boy Models L and LA. The R was still a single-speed tractor, yet its design was much more effective than that of its predecessors. This tractor featured an improved engine design, one that would eventually become synonymous with the John Deere name: the horizontal two-cylinder engine. The R's engine started out having only a 5.5x7-inch bore and stroke, but the bore was increased twice, both in increments of one-half inch. Thus, by the end of its production, the Waterloo Boy R had a 6.5x7-inch bore and stroke that provided 465 cubic inches of displacement, producing around 12 drawbar horsepower and 25 belt horsepower when operating at 750 rpm. Other changes occurred to the R over this time period, including a switch to

This experimental tractor is one of the many styles that appeared before the final design for the Model D tractor. Note, however, how this model more closely resemble the future Model D than it does the Waterloo Boy Models R and N. *Deere & Company Archives*

Precursors to a Legend

Without the Waterloo Gasoline Engine Company, it is entirely possible that the Model D as we know it never would have come into being. That Waterloo, Iowa, company started producing its Waterloo Boy lightweight tractors in the 1913 model year, and that series eventually evolved into the Model D.

The first of the Waterloo Boy "Light" tractors was the Waterloo Boy Model L, introduced in 1913. A single-speed tractor, the L had only three wheels, with only one rear-wheel receiving power. The Waterloo Gasoline Engine Traction Company also produced a four-wheeled unit based on the L; this new model, the Waterloo Boy LA, had two driven wheels. These two tractor models saw only limited production during the 1913 and 1914 model years. Also referred to

a detachable cylinder head. To denote the improved (or even specialized) versions of the tractor, the company implemented a system of adding a letter suffix to the R designation. In all, 13 different letters were used, ranging from A to M. Production of the Waterloo Boy R continued until the 1919 model year, the final configuration being the RM, which was the first to use the engine with the 6.5x7-inch bore and stroke.

Upon the introduction of a new version of the Waterloo Boy in the 1917 model year, the Waterloo Gasoline Engine Company decided to simply designate it the Model N. The letter "N" followed directly in sequence after the style M of the R Series Waterloo Boys, only now the "R" had been dropped and the "N" was the actual model designation of the tractor. Interestingly, the R Series Waterloo Boys continued in production until the 1919 model year, being produced simultaneously with the improved Model N.

It's no surprise that the N looked very similar to the R, making use of the same chassis design. The primary improvement of the new N, however, was its use of a two-speed transmission. Still, the same horizontal two-cylinder engine with the 6.5x7-inch bore and stroke was employed, and the rated rpm was still 750. Even more significant is that the advertised horsepower ratings of the N were proven, as the Waterloo Boy N was the very first tractor to be subjected to the tractor tests at the University of Nebraska. In Test 1, which ran from March 31 to April 9 of 1920, the N produced over 25 brake horsepower and nearly 16 drawbar horsepower in the maximum load tests.

In 1918, when the Waterloo Boy Models R and N were in production, Deere & Company approached the Waterloo Gasoline Engine Company about purchasing the company. On March 14, 1918, the purchase was made, propelling Deere & Company to a full-line status with this addition of tractor and engine production. Not only was Deere now producing tractors for the American market, but the company was also exporting them to places as far away as Puerto Rico, Peru, South Africa, and France. Deere continued production of the Model R until the 1919 model year, and production of the Model N lasted until 1924.

Fortunately, when Deere purchased the Waterloo Gasoline Engine Company, the ideas, research, and developments of that company came along with it. Experimentation

on a new version of the Waterloo Boy—with drastic changes in both appearance and design—had been under way since at least 1917, with the new tractors bearing the designation "Model A." It is unclear how many experimental tractors Waterloo actually assembled at that early date. However, in all, Deere Archives indicates that seven tractors, serial-numbered 100 to 106, were eventually made under that experimental designation, though it is unclear if all were made by Waterloo itself or if some were produced by Deere, as well.

After Deere had acquired the Waterloo Gasoline Engine Company, it sped up the experimentation that Waterloo had begun. Deere rolled out seven such tractors—bearing serial numbers 200 to 206—by the end of 1921, with units being documented by Deere's Serial Number Registers as having been shipped as early as September 19 of that year. Though these units are also listed under the "Model A" in Deere's Serial Number Registers, there is some speculation that these tractors were actually called "Style (or Model) Bs."

Following the 1921 experimental tractors, 12 more units were made starting in 1922, with the first units appearing as early as July 31, 1922. This last set of experimental tractors bore serial numbers 300 to 311, and even though these tractors are listed under the "Model A" designation in Deere's serial-number records, some people suspect that these tractors might have been referred to as "Style (or Model) Cs."

Regular Production Begins

In 1923, those two-dozen experimental tractors finally paid off, as Deere began regular production of its Model D early that summer, with serial number 30401 being the first. It was shipped on May 30, 1923, to Deere's San Francisco branch. Interestingly, though, a tractor numbered 401 (likely the same tractor as 30401) was reportedly shipped to the Waterloo Implement Company on April 16, 1923.

The D was viewed as a big improvement over the Waterloo Boy models, and for a variety of reasons. For one, the new D could be started by turning the flywheel by hand without the use of a starting crank. That feature alone set the D apart from the majority of the other tractors on the market, as most at that time still required a hand crank to be employed to start them. Another unique feature of the D was its frameless design. It didn't need a frame, as the crankcase was cast in with the main case, the cylinder blocks bolted directly onto the front

This collection of four photos shows various angles of the Waterloo Boy experimental models that eventually led to the Model D of 1923. This tractor resembles the Model D from the rear in particular. These photos were taken around 1919, close to the time that Deere purchased the Waterloo Gasoline Engine Company. *Deere & Company Archives*

of the crankcase, and the front axle assembly connected with them. The use of live rear axles on the D also gave it an edge over the exposed gearing of the drive wheels on the Waterloo Boy, as well.

The Model D wasn't entirely different from the Waterloo Boy Model N, however. For instance, the Model D started production using a 6.5x7-inch engine with 465 cubic inches of displacement, just like the Waterloo Boy N. The D's rated rpm was 800 instead of 750, however. Also like the Waterloo Boy Model N, the Model D John Deere featured a two-speed transmission. Forward speeds of 2.5 and 3.25 miles per hour were provided on both the Waterloo Boy N and the John Deere D. The D's single reverse speed of 2 miles per hour, however, was one-quarter mile per hour slower than that of the Waterloo Boy N. Fenders and steel wheels came as standard equipment on the Model D, just as they had on its predecessor.

The 1923 Models

Deere produced a total of 50 Model Ds in the 1923 model year, with serial numbers ranging from 30401 to 30450. Those tractors are very easy to distinguish from later-model Ds, having a number of unique features. These tractors featured "built-up" or "weldment"-style front axles, and the sides of the radiators had four rounded-corner square holes. Other features included steering wheels with four holes notched out of each of the spokes.

Toward the end of the 1923 model year, Deere issued two different Decisions that ultimately made the 1923 models so unique. First, on August 4, 1923, the company issued Decision D-80, which called for the removal of the four openings in

each of the D's D55R radiator sides, a move that was done in order to simplify the design of the tractor. The second Decision, number D-196, appeared on November 2, 1923. It eliminated the original front axle of the D. Decision D-196 states, "To provide an axle that will stand up in the field, we will adopt a malleable casting to replace the old style built up job." It also indicates that the new front axle would be interchangeable with the old one, meaning that it is possible that one could find a 1923 D today that has the later-style (though far more common) front axle. After the D's initial production year yielded only 50 units, it was no surprise that the Model D built up a lot of steam in its production in the following years.

The 1924 Models

The 1924 Model D tractors benefited from the production changes Deere made at the beginning of that year, including the new cast-iron front axle. Production in the 1924 model year ranged from serial number 30451 to 31303.

The Serial Number Registers at Deere Archives indicate that there were a few 1924 model tractors that were extra-special. Tractors 30682, 30687, 30692, 30699, and 30707 all are denoted as being equipped with a "special steering shaft." Also, tractor 31112 is listed as having been fitted with "Special Pistons 6.491"; unfortunately, no other particulars are known regarding these interesting features.

Partway through the 1924 model year, Deere addressed the problem they were having with the large size of the flywheel on the Model D. Apparently, some operators experienced problems with the left front wheel running into the flywheel when turning in that direction. Thus, Deere decided to reduce

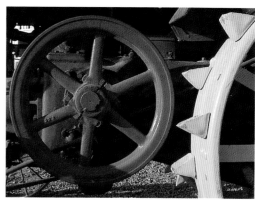

Above: Unique to the early Model Ds is the spoked flywheel. The Model D started production with a 26-inch flywheel as seen in this photo, but a smaller version replaced it in late 1924. Only about 880 "Spoker" Ds used this 26-inch spoked flywheel.

Left: Only 24 tractors before the end of the 1924 model year, at serial number 31280, Deere replaced the original 26-inch flywheel with a smaller 24-inch flywheel. That flywheel remained in use until serial number 36249, when a solid flywheel was used. Deere produced nearly 4,900 "Spoker" Ds using the 24-inch spoked flywheel.

the diameter of the flywheel from 26 to 24 inches. This change first took place as a regular practice on tractor 31280, and the spoked flywheel would stay the same size until it was replaced by a solid design two years later.

The 1925 Models

Production for the 1925 model year started with serial number 31304 and ended just over 4,000 numbers later, with serial number 35308. However, 1925 D production did not include all of those serial numbers, as nearly a hundred of them—ranging from 31321 to 31412—were set aside for use on the 1924 Waterloo Boy Model N tractors. This was done because Deere had underestimated the number of Model Ns it would need to produce before the model was totally discontinued.

A handful of the 1925 Model Ds were the first tractors bearing the John Deere name to be shipped overseas. The earliest known exported Ds were serial numbers 32880,

The Model D John Deere has long stood as one of the most notable tractors in Deere & Company history. Derived from the Waterloo Boy, the D was the first letter-series tractor in Deere's line. The letter series would ultimately be replaced by the New Generation tractors similar to the one n the background.

Perhaps the most desirable Spoker Ds are the 1923 model tractors, yet those are among the most difficult Model D series versions to find. Still, almost any Deere collector would love to have any Spoker D in his or her collection. Those later-model Spoker Ds can be quickly distinguished by their full, solid radiator sides and other features that were improved at the beginning of the 1924 model year.

32881, 32883, 32898, 32909, and 32915, all of which were shipped to Bulgaria in May, according to the Deere Serial Number Registers for the D. Other 1925 Model Ds that are recorded as exported include the following:

Other Exported 1925 Model Ds	
32984	
33050	34140
33055	34293
33057	34294
33061	34305
34062	34332
34080	34334
34112	34670
34113	34672
34114	34673

Several 1925 Model Ds have interesting notes written beside their numbers in the Serial Number Registers at Deere Archives. For instance, tractors 32918 through 32920 and 32925 through 32929 are all noted as having been drilled for power take-off shafts. Also, tractors 33525, 33573, 33578, 33579, 33581 to 33584, and 33643 are all noted as having the "Old style spline gear cover."

The "Spoker Ds" End Production

Though the "Spoker Ds" are popular today with collectors, Deere opted to eliminate the spoked flywheel from these tractors partway through the 1926 model year. The Model D number 36249 was the first to be regularly equipped with the new, solid flywheel. One earlier tractor, number 35891, had also been fitted with a solid flywheel on an experimental basis.

The Model D Undergoes a Host of Changes

True, the Model D changed considerably in its first few years of production. But the changes had only just begun at the time that the D received the new solid flywheel. Here are some of the most notable changes that occurred from that time until the model received an overall facelift in 1939.

A Boost in Engine Size

Late in the 1927 model year, at serial number 53388, Deere increased the bore of the D from 6-1/2 to 6-3/4 inches, a change that resulted in an increased horsepower rating. Tractor #60250 tackled the Nebraska Tractor Tests, pounding out an impressive maximum load brake horsepower of 36.98, up considerably from the 30.4 horsepower delivered in the 1924 tests. Similarly, the maximum load drawbar horsepower was up exactly six units to 28.53 horsepower. Although

the D retained its original 15–27 rated horsepower, the tractor was capable of doing more than it had before.

The "Exhibit A" Model Ds

In 1928, Deere & Company decided it was time to consider some major changes for the venerable Model D. Ninety-six consecutively serial-numbered experimental Model Ds—ranging from number 67501 to 67596—acted upon those ideas, and Deere denoted them as "Exhibit A" tractors. Adorning these special tractors were a new three-speed transmission, a power take-off that was mounted inside the main case (as opposed to the original optional unit that ran alongside the main case to the back of the tractor), a new drag link-type steering system, Timken roller bearings, and a larger-capacity fuel tank. Of equal importance was the increased power of these Ds, tractors that could now pound out approximately 40 belt horsepower. Enthusiasts can identify these tractors by the serial numbers and the letter "X" that precedes those numbers.

Flat-Spoked Front Wheels

A number of the Model Ds produced during the 1929 model year received new flat-spoked front steel wheels. They only appeared on the D in that model year, though they were not used on every tractor during that year. Thus, if you find a flat-spoked front wheel for the Model D, odds are it came from a 1929 tractor.

The "Exhibit B" Tractors

The "Exhibit A" tractors did not cause immediate changes to the regular-production Model D. Production continued as usual, but by the summer of 1930, Deere was still itching to make more out of the D. At that time, the

The Model D entered production with steel wheels as standard equipment. Even though rubber tires would become more popular into the 1930s as options, steel wheels delivered the D's power to the ground effectively. Rear steel extension rims were also available to provide added traction when needed.

decision was made to manufacture 50 more experimental Ds to help satisfy that urge, but these units would have even more changes than did the "Exhibit A" tractors. The new experimental models would also boast a faster governed rpm, up to 900 from 800, plus an upright exhaust stack, a bigger air cleaner, and a new belt pulley. These 50 tractors—serial-numbered from B107001 to B107050—were known as "Exhibit B" tractors. It is important to note that a number of the tractors in the "Exhibit B" serial-number range are listed as "Scrapped" in the Serial Number Registers of Deere & Company. Such scrapped tractors include the following:

Scrapped "Exhibit B" Model Ds

107001	107041
107033	107043
107034	107047
107040	107048

Almost all of the new features of the "Exhibit B" tractors proved most effective, so Deere was pleased. Thus, for the 1931 model year, the regular-production Model D incorporated almost all of those new features into its design. The changes that occurred at this time have been referred to as the single-largest change in the Model D in all of its history, possibly even surpassing the later change from unstyled to styled.

Fine-Tuning the Model D

Decision 5000 of September 1934 called for the adoption of a new three-speed transmission for the Model D. This new transmission provided a road gear of 5 miles per hour, and it was first installed as regular equipment on D 119100 on November 22, 1934.

On May 8, 1935, Deere issued its Decision 5482, which stated that 100 Model Ds would be fitted with improved rear axles and drive-wheel assemblies. The rear axles would be strengthened over the previous design by an increased diameter, from 3 inches to 3-1/4 inches at the outer bearings. Accompanying Deere documents indicate that these changes were first put in effect on all Model Ds in the block of serial numbers from 123100 to 123200. Deere's Serial Number Registers show a flurry of activity to tractors in that serial-number block, indicating that tractor 123188 was scrapped, while the following tractors were ultimately rebuilt:

Rebuilt Model Ds
That Were Originally Fitted with Special Rear Axles

123101	123171
123124	123172
123135	123177
123142	123182
123148	123190
123165	123194
123170	123198

It is also interesting to note that tractor 123184 is listed in the Serial Number Registers as being an "Industrial Model w/12.75x28 Rear and 7.50x18 Front [tires]."

The Model D Rebuilds

Nearly one thousand tractors were built after the last D received the experimental rear-axle housings and drive wheels. There were a number of Model Ds that were ultimately rebuilt and received new serial numbers. Though the reason for this change is unclear, it is possible that it is related to the changes made to tractors 123100 to 123200. The tractors affected were interspersed between serial numbers 124198 and 125074. To kick off 1936 production, Deere rebuilt those tractors into regular-production tractors with new numbers ranging from 125079 to 125250. After Deere scrapped serial numbers 125251 to 125290, another large group of tractors were rebuilt and renumbered from 125291 to 125413, with the exception of tractor 125330, which appears to have not been rebuilt from a previous tractor.

The Specialized Model Ds

Though always of the standard-tread design, the Model D John Deere appeared in various specialized forms at various stages in its production. Many of these tractors were produced prior to the 1939 styling of the tractor.

The Industrial Model Ds

As early as 1925, John Deere started producing the Model D in a specialized version for use in industrial applications. However, at that time, the model was not given a special designation; the tractors were simply well-modified

The D had the longest production run of any Deere tractor, so it's not surprising that it also was the model with the longest production in unstyled form. The D didn't receive styled lines until partway through the 1939 model year, unlike the majority of Deere's other core models, which were styled at the beginning of that year.

agricultural tractors. Typically, these units featured solid rubber tires and 28-tooth sprockets for the chain-driven axle assembly, which gave them a higher gear ratio.

John Deere advertising literature from 1926 for the "John Deere Industrial Tractor" indicates that this model variation came with 40x8-inch rear and 24x3.5-inch front wheels with plain rubber tires. Also indicated was that the regular sprockets for the chain-driven axle assembly could be replaced by either 28-tooth sprockets or 22-tooth sprockets. The former increased the tractors' speeds to 3 and 4 miles per hour, whereas the latter boosted forward speeds to 3.75 and 5 miles per hour. The 22-tooth sprockets were supposed to be used only with the available 50-inch wheels. The literature also indicated that wheel weight sets (with two weights per set) were available in packages of 400, 500, 1,800, or 1,900 pounds. Additionally, 40x5-inch rear extension wheels with plain rubber tires were optional.

Deere decided that this industrialized version of the Model D deserved its own model designation. So, the company issued Decision 5731, which outlined the features of the "new" model—the Model DI. Stylistically, the DI would be painted "Highway Yellow" with stenciling in black. Furthermore, the tractor would be fitted with low-pressure

pneumatic tires with special 900-pound rear-wheel weights. Additionally, the units would make use of a 28-tooth sprocket and drive assembly, a "brake control extension," and an extension for the swinging drawbar. The first DI to be regularly affected by Decision 5731 was tractor 125581, which was produced two days before Christmas in 1935. Listed here are earlier serial-numbered tractors that are also listed as Model DIs. Note that these tractors had also been fitted with the improved rear axles.

Earlier Model DIs	
123172	123184
123174	123185
123176	123188
123179	123196
123182	123197

Today, DIs are very popular with collectors, as not too many of them were assembled. The Serial Number Registers at Deere & Company Archives list the following tractors as Model DIs, as well, being indicated as such by the 124 model code.

Model DI Serial Numbers	
126824 (hand-control brakes)	129084
126825 (hand-control brakes)	129365
127052 (scrapped)	131316
127083	131317
127084 (experimental shipped "export")	131318
127085	131319
127086	131347
127087	131348
128596	148838
129083	150118

Earlier Ds Receiving Rear Hand Brakes	
125583	
125584	125587
125585	125589
125586	125590

Deere increased the options list for the DI model by issuing two closely numbered Decisions in the winter of 1936. The first approved item was low-pressure dual rear tires, which Decision 6107 of January 30, 1936, authorized. The first tractor to benefit from that Decision was 127451, a tractor produced on April 6, 1936. The second Decision—number 6109—came on February 11, 1936, though it was reportedly put in effect the day before that. It allowed for optional rear-wheel handbrakes to be installed on the DI, and the first affected tractor was 126415. Deere documents also indicate that the following earlier tractors received that feature, as well:

Even though the basic Model D was styled for the 1939 model year, Deere continued to produce the similar Model DI in the unstyled form after that time. No records indicate that any Model DIs were ever styled by Deere. Tractor 150118, which was shipped on March 5, 1941, is the last known Model DI.

The Model D Hawkeye Motor Patrol

One of the rarest attachments one can find on the Model D is the Hawkeye Motor Patrol road maintainer. This maintainer, which the Hawkeye Maintainer Company of Waterloo, Iowa, produced, was installed on special versions of the Model D sometime in the 1929 model year and continued on a small scale until perhaps as late as the 1931 model year. Unfortunately, little is known about the actual production of these units, although it is known that these units used different wheels than were ordinarily used on the Model D and that Deere assembled these Ds without platforms or fenders.

The Model D Hawkeye Motor Patrol John Deere tractor served well in the capacity of road maintenance. Unfortunately, none of these units are known to still be in existence. *Deere & Company Archives*

The Model D Crawlers

In the summer of 1930, Deere produced two Model Ds that were far different from anything that had ever come before. Little is known about these tractors, but Deere denoted them as crawler-type tractors in the Serial Number Registers. Serial number 107039 was the first, and it also received the notation "New DX23." The other tractor—serial number 107042—also received the notation "New DX24." It is important to note that both of these very special tractors are also "Exhibit B" tractors according to the serial numbers.

The last tractor with the special rear-axle assemblies, 123200, left Deere bound for the Caterpillar Tractor Company of Peoria, Illinois, on October 7, 1935. The tractor was then rebuilt into a Model DI on May 22, 1936, receiving a new serial number—128596. Deere also shipped D123368 to Caterpillar in late June 1935. However, it is unclear if either of these tractors received crawler modifications.

Not much later than the Caterpillar shipments, the Lindeman Power Implement Company of Yakima, Washington, fitted a track system onto a few Model Ds. Unfortunately, no information is available on the serial numbers of the tractors affected.

The Exported Model Ds

Even though exports of the Model D started as early as 1925, the number of exports remained fairly low the first few years. In 1926, exports continued to Bulgaria, but Ds were also being exported to a variety of other locations by year's end, including Nairobi and Russia.

The Nairobi shipments are rather interesting, especially beginning in the 1927 model year. Almost all of the tractors shipped to Nairobi in that model year were also fitted with special "Silichrome Valves," according to the Serial Number Registers. These included tractors 46145 to 46147 and 46598 to 46601.

Other tractors with special valve notations in the Registers include 44031 to 44038 and 46602 to 46606, though not all of these tractors went overseas. Tractors from the last batch were alternately shipped to both Nairobi and to Deere's Kansas City branch. Still other notable tractors are 44512 to 44520, along with 44644 and 44647, all of which are noted as having "valves and Heavy Diff." One tractor, 46199, was shipped to South Africa, and it is noted as having both the silichrome exhaust valves and the 28-tooth sprockets, the latter being common on industrial versions of the D.

The number of locations for exports increased steadily over the next few years. Shipments to Czechoslovakia began as early as 1927. Also, the D was also exported to Buenos Aires and Hamburg, Germany, in 1928. Furthermore, shipments were made to Santiago; Budapest, Hungary; Sydney, Australia; and even Egypt in 1929. It is also interesting to note that the number of exports to Russia skyrocketed

beginning in that year. Just a few of the many big blocks of serial numbers shipped to Russia include numbers 95367 to 95899, 97500 to 97517, and 97519 to 99499.

Another big batch of exports took place, including tractors from serial numbers 107439 to 109943. Each of those tractors (except 108075, which was scrapped) was shipped overseas. Many of those tractors were also exported to Russia, but some tractors found their way to other destinations, including Rio de Janeiro, Tunis, Buenos Aires, Czechoslovakia, and even Casablanca, Morocco. It is interesting to note, as well, that of the last 1,200 tractors in this serial-number block, some that were listed as being exported went to New York. Possibly those tractors went to new overseas destinations from there.

The "Row-Crop" Model Ds

On March 17, 1936, Deere published Decision 6198 to allow 35 sets of skeleton steel wheels to be used on the Model D Series tractors. Though it is unclear which tractors actually received this special option, these tractors have come to be known as "row-crop" Model Ds.

The Hot-Manifold Ds

During the 1937 model year, Deere produced a few special Model Ds that were fitted with a special "hot" manifold that made use in colder climates easier, or, in some cases, possible. A handful of Ds bound for Calgary, Alberta, Canada, received this special manifold, and the following tractors are listed as having such in the Serial Number Registers of Deere & Company:

Model Ds Fitted with Hot Manifold	
133457	133560
133459	133655
133460	133658
133461	133661

Tractors intended for use in the United States were also fitted with a similar manifold, and the Serial Number Registers of Deere & Company indicate that the following tractors featured that manifold and were bound for Deere's Kansas City branch:

Model Ds Fitted with Special Manifold
133654
133656
133657
133659
133660

The Styled Model D

The Model D participated in the styling revolution that many of Deere's tractor models underwent during the 1939 model year. Deere had previously approached Henry Dreyfuss & Associates with the task of styling its tractors. Dreyfuss accepted the challenge of making Deere's world-famous tractors look more modern. The stalwart D, while not the first tractor to be experimented with stylistically, certainly received special attention from Dreyfuss, and for good reason: the D had a different look from any of the other basic models in Deere's line (i.e., the Models A, B, G, L, and the new H).

Deere authorized production of the new styled D more than a year before production actually began. The initial Decision—numbered 8200—was dated February 15, 1938, but the first styled D—serial number 143800—did not see the light of day until March 31, 1939. It is important to note that the Model D was NOT stylized at the beginning of the 1939 model year. Nineteen thirty-nine production began some 1,500 serial numbers earlier, and all of those 1939 tractors between serial numbers 142300 and 143800 were unstyled. The newly styled D featured a vertically slatted grille (whereas the other styled tractors in Deere's line had received horizontally slatted grilles) and came standard with full fenders. The hood design of the D was consistent with the rest of Deere's newly styled line.

Initially, steel wheels were still standard equipment on the styled Model D, so it's no surprise that rubber tires were a very popular option at the start of production. In fact, the styled D's option list looked very much like that of the unstyled D. There was one very important addition to the options list: electric starting.

The Model D was available in only two versions: the basic agricultural Model D and the similar industrially oriented Model DI. Orchard equipment was available as options on the Model D as well, but there was never a Model DO orchard tractor as such.

The D was most often used for plowing fields, but it was also very effective and popular power for belt-driven equipment. A number of Model Ds still do those activities at tractor shows around the world.

Overall, when compared to the history of the unstyled Model D, the history of the styled Model D seems unexciting. No huge changes took place, so the tractor remained much the same from 1939 until the end of production in 1953. Oddly enough, perhaps the most interesting of the styled Ds were the last ones produced. Ordinary factory production of the Model D ended with serial number 191578 in late March 1953. But that tractor was NOT the last Model D to see the light of day. In fact, there were 92 Model Ds that saw the light of day before they were even completed. Those 92 tractors—serial numbers 191579 to 191670—were actually built out on the street. Thus, these tractors became known as "Streeter Ds." Deere built them on the street because the factory was undergoing renovations.

The Legend Ends Production

The number "31" has a dual significance for the Model D John Deere. In 1931, the D underwent possibly more changes than it ever had before. Those changes helped to solidify the D as a venerable and effective tractor that remained reliable and popular throughout the years. But 31 has another meaning for the D that is even more special: the D was in production for 31 model years, with production occurring every year from 1923 to 1953. The last model D—serial number 191670—completed its assembly on July 3, 1953, more than 30 years after the first D was produced.

The John Deere D holds the record for the longest production span of any tractor model. It was one of the most successful tractors in all of Deere & Company's history. Amazingly, its production covered all but one year, the last, of John Deere's letter-series tractor production. The only letter-series Deere tractor that was produced in the model year in which the D was not, was the Model R, which fittingly is the subject of the last chapter of this book. The Model D was an amazing tractor, and it has an amazing history. For collectors, the legend lives on!

Chapter Two

The Model C
and GP Series

In the early to mid-1920s, a variety of tractor companies were making moves to produce tractors that would work well in the cultivation of row crops. In 1925, the same year that International Harvester submitted its Farmall tractor to be tested at the University of Nebraska, Deere started working on an idea for its first general-purpose tractor. Deere intended the new model to fill the need for a tractor that could both plow, as most standard-tread tractors were designed for, and cultivate, as most row-crop or cultivator-type tractors were designed for.

Deere engineers worked diligently on this new project, and their first tractor became known as the "All Crop." Wooden models of the proposed tractor were constructed, and the engineers considered implement attachment and a power-lift system to lift and lower the attached implements. Also, even though crop clearance for such a tractor was a major concern, Deere didn't sacrifice the safety of the tractor for additional clearance. Indeed, the All Crop had been planned to have 28 inches of crop clearance, but for stability's sake, crop clearance was reduced to 24 inches even before a working example was assembled. The first working All Crop took to the fields for additional experimentation in the summer of 1926. By October, at least three All Crop tractors had been assembled. Deere spent much time using the All Crop tractor in the field with a wide array of attachments, as that was the work place where the most development needed to occur to achieve Deere's goals.

Opposite: The Model GP always came standard on steel wheels. However, rubber tires did eventually become available for these units. The majority of the Model GPs left the factory on steel wheels, but a number were converted by farmers later.

Deere's answer to the row-crop question: the Model C. With this model, which soon evolved into the Model GP, Deere was well on its way to finding the ideal general-purpose tractor.

The Model C Production Begins

Deere & Company decided to move forward with production of its new model, dropping the All Crop title and renaming it the Model C. Decision C-3, issued on June 11, 1927, approved production of this new model.

The Model C first entered production on August 1, 1927, starting with serial number 200001. Production continued until January 18, 1928, ending with number 200110. By that time, only 75 Model Cs had been produced, as several

The Model C featured no stacks of any kind, making this model turn people's heads. Many people use the GP's stacks as a means of identifying that model as opposed to the C.

Deere designed its experimental All Crop and, consequently, the Model C as a three-row tractor. Thus, one row ran beneath the tractor, while the remaining rows ran just outside the rear wheels.

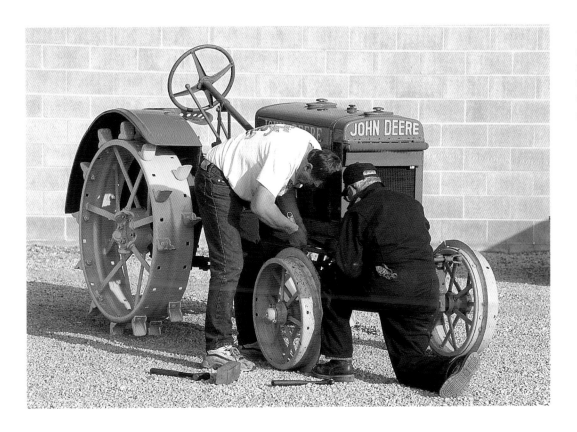

serial numbers were not used. Those unused numbers include the following:

Unused Early Model C Numbers
200009
200010
200024
200070 to 200079
200081 to 200098
200100
200101
200104
200105

Decision C-200 of January 24, 1928, stated that all Cs built before that date were to be returned and rebuilt to fit new specifications for the model. It is unclear as to exactly why Deere decided that the Model Cs produced to that time needed to be recalled. Almost all of those original 75 tractors were indeed returned to the factory in the winter of 1927–1928, rebuilt, renumbered, and then sent back to their owners. As directed by Decision C-200, the first number used on the revised Model C was 200111, picking up right where initial production of the C had left off.

Tractor 200111, originally numbered 200015, came back out of the factory on March 15, 1928, starting 1928 production. Deere then shipped tractor 200112 to Omaha on October 19, 1928, to be tested at the University of Nebraska. The unit performed in Test 153 from October 22 to October 29, 1928, pounding out 24.97 brake horsepower under maximum load. This tractor was a Model C, even though these results are often said to be that of a Model GP.

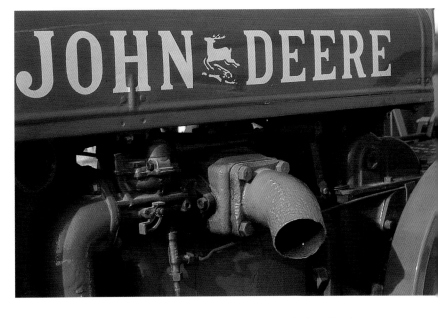

The tie rod of the Model C's front end ran in front of the axle assembly. Owners of any tractor should make sure that such pivot points on their tractors, even if just taken to shows, are lubricated properly and at regular intervals.

One noted difference between the Model C and its replacement, the Model GP, exists in their steering wheels. The C used a wooden steering wheel rim, whereas the GP used the more traditional cast-iron wheel.

Since the wooden steering wheels originally used on the Model C are over 70 years old, most of them have deteriorated into nonexistence. Thus, getting one of these wheels formed can be a challenge for a Model C collector.

The exhaust pipe of the Model C appears on the flywheel side of the tractor. This simple exhaust outlet didn't make use of a muffler, an item that wouldn't become popular on tractors for another 10-plus years.

The Serial Number Registers of Deere & Company reveal much about the Model C production, including which later serial-numbered models were rebuilt from which original units. Here are the numbers of all known original Model Cs and the numbers they received after being rebuilt:

Rebuilt Model Cs

200002 rebuilt into 200122	200028 rebuilt into 200133	200054 rebuilt into 200120
200006 rebuilt into 200124	200029 rebuilt into 200135	200055 rebuilt into 200137
200007 rebuilt into 200157	200032 rebuilt into 200129	200056 rebuilt into 200119
200008 rebuilt into 200182	200033 rebuilt into 200117	200057 rebuilt into 200125
200013 rebuilt into 200134	200034 rebuilt into 200178	200059 rebuilt into 200143
200014 rebuilt into 200128	200036 rebuilt into 200126	200060 rebuilt into 200159
200015 rebuilt into 200111	200037 rebuilt into 200150	200063 rebuilt into 200160
200017 rebuilt into 200144	200040 rebuilt into 200163	200066 rebuilt into 200166
200019 rebuilt into 200156	200043 rebuilt into 200114	200068 rebuilt into 200170
200020 rebuilt into 200139	200050 rebuilt into 200116	200069 rebuilt into 200168
200025 rebuilt into 200148	200051 rebuilt into 200138	
200026 rebuilt into 200146	200053 rebuilt into 200141	

Even though the Model GP came standard with steel wheels, many farmers felt that the optional rubber tires were a worthy investment.

Did You Say "D" or "C"?

Odds are that this question has been asked at least once in relation to the Model C John Deere. When considering the fact that the C first entered production at the start of August 1927, the C had been around for about eight months by the time April 1928 came around. By that time, though, Deere documents indicate that the Model C's designation had been problematic. Apparently, there was a problem when dealers would call in orders for tractors at this time, as the two Deere tractor models had designations that sounded very similar. Deere considered several options to remedy that problem.

One way that Deere could have dealt with the confusion over model designations was to simply designate the models based on their rated horsepower, a practice that was

common with other tractor manufacturers at the time. The Model C could have been redesignated the Model 10-20, and the Model D could have been redesignated the Model 15-27. It wouldn't have been that big a deal, though, as the D had long been referred to as the 15-27 in advertising literature (even as late as 1927) and in other places. However, by this time Deere felt it was important to distinguish themselves from their competitors. After all, there was already a Mc-Cormick-Deering Model 10-20 on the market, and that tractor was vastly different from Deere's 10-20-horsepower Model C. Deere ultimately decided to not designate the models on the basis of horsepower, and the prevalence of the letter designations became very important in the years to come.

Deere could also have dealt with the problem by calling their two models by nicknames of sorts. The proposed

nicknames for this model included the "Farmrite" and "Powerfarmer." However, in the end, Deere didn't feel that assigning these nicknames to their tractors was the right move to make, so neither name was used.

The Model GP Is Born

In the end, Deere & Company decided to redesignate the Model C with another letter designation. Furthermore, it was decided to give this model a letter designation that stood exactly for what it was: a general-purpose tractor. Thus, the Model GP designation was born, "GP" standing for General Purpose. Deere built the last Model C, number 200202, in April 1928, just one short month after production had resumed. Serial numbers 200203 to 200210 were never used, and the

Model GP designation went into effect beginning with tractor 200211.

The GP John Deere in many ways resembled the Model C. The GP used the same engine, starting production using a 5-3/4-inch bore and a 6-inch stroke. Rated at 900 rpm, this 312-cubic-inch two-cylinder, L-head engine produced a maximum load brake horsepower rating of 24.97 and a maximum load drawbar rating of 17.24 horsepower. Deere chose to keep the advertised rating of this tractor at 10–20 nonetheless.

Like the Model C, the GP resembled the Model D at first glance. However, the GP's chassis design was quite different from that of the D. The most important difference was the GP's use of drop box-type rear axles. This feature allowed for greater crop clearance beneath the rear end of the tractor.

Perhaps the most well-known derivative of the GP that wasn't chassis-based is the GP with crossover manifold. These units are highly collectible and easily distinguishable from the flywheel side.

Above: This tractor, serial number 200109, is a Model C. Note that this tractor lacks air stacks, as stacks did not appear on the C.

Above right: This 1929 GP, serial number 203901, has an air intake stack, unlike the Model C. Note that the exhaust system had not changed by this time, however.

Right: This 1930 model GP crossover, serial number 222357, shows how the crossover manifold changed the look of these tractors. The long "crossover" is easily distinguishable on this tractor.

Also beneficial for the cultivation of row-crops, the arched front axle on the GP set it apart from the straight front axle of the D.

The Model GP Tricycle

The GP in its original form did have some limitations when it came to cultivation of row-crops, including the fact that it couldn't work with just any set of cultivators, listers, or planters. This was mainly due to the fact that the GP was a three-row tractor. The GP wasn't as successful on its own as Deere would have liked, so the company decided to try to address its shortcomings. Deere decided that it would convert their GP into a row-crop–type tractor of the tricycle-type configuration.

Thus, on November 12, 1928, Deere & Company issued Decision C656 calling for the production of 50 GP Tricycle tractors. The first was to be built by December 15 and were all to be finished by January 15, 1929. Deere documents indicate that this decision wasn't put into effect until January 19, 1929, affecting tractor 202356 and all tractors from 202380 to 202428. Furthermore, the Serial Number Registers of Deere & Company indicate that the following GP tractors were built as GP Tricycles:

GP Tricycle Serial Numbers

200264	200377	200458	203989
200272	200400	201301	204072
200287	200403	202356	204077 (68-inch tread)
200297	200406	202380 to 202428	204172
200346	200431	203874 (68-inch tread)	204213
200366	200438	203970	

This experimental unit, which eventually led to the GP Tricycle and the GPWT, is among the earliest tricycle front-end tractors. Note the absence of the "JOHN DEERE" lettering on the radiator top tank. *Deere & Company Archives*

Previous page: *The original GP was not successful as a row-crop tractor. The company introduced the GP Tricycle to combat the problems. This tractor, a GP Wide Tread, is one of the beneficiaries of Deere's work on that model.*

Much like the Farmall Regular, the John Deere GPWT used drop-box rear axles and a full-width drawbar. The full-width drawbar allowed farmers to attach implements in a wide array of fixed positions to satisfy different operations.

The GP Tricycle used the same basic rear end as that of the original GP, but the Tricycle used a dual-wheeled, narrow-set "tricycle" front end instead of the wide, arched front axle used on the original model. Furthermore, the front end on the GP Tricycle was set ahead of the radiator of the tractor, made possible by extending the front end of the tractor. The GP Tricycle didn't feature fenders, and that alone makes the model look vastly different from the GP, which included fenders as standard equipment.

The Model GP Wide Tread

Deere's Decision C699 of January 7, 1929, reads "To better describe the uses for which the Tricycle Tractor is intended, we will change the name to General Purpose Wide Tread Tractor" and was to be made effective immediately. So was born the Model GP Wide Tread, and it began production in the 1929 model year at serial number 40000, starting a new, exclusive serial-number run.

Deere redesignated and renumbered a few Model GP Tricycles as GP Wide Treads according to the Serial Number Registers. The converted GP Tricycles and their resultant GP-WT numbers are as follows:

GP Tricycles Converted into GP-WTs

201301 became 403266	209486 became 400057
201382 became 402225	209499 became 400058
209280 became 400052	209610 became 400059
209283 became 400053	209611 became 400060
209294 became 400054	209957 became 400063
209300 became 400055	209963 became 400064
209408 became 400056	

The GP Wide Tread Series P

Deere had for some time been toying with the idea of a modified version of the Tricycle version of the GP tractor that would be better suited to the cultivation of potatoes. Potato cultivation called for a tractor with a 68-inch rear tread, and Deere experimented on at least two GP Tricycle tractors in the spring of 1929, narrowing their rear treads to 68 inches. The earliest known such GP Tricycle outlined in Deere's Serial Number Registers was serial number 203784, which is noted as a "Tricycle, 68 inch" version. The other known tractor was number 204077, which is marked as a "Tricycle 68 inch special" in the Serial Number Registers. It was completed in late March 1929, meaning that it actually was completed before 203784. Interestingly, 203784 is chronologically the next-to-the-last GP Tricycle to be completed; it was finished only one day before GP Tricycle 203970, which was finished on April 27, 1929.

As indicated above, GP Tricycle production terminated once Deere redesignated the model as the Model GP Wide Tread. Thus, if the 68-inch versions of the old GP Tricycle were found to be successful, then production of that type of tractor was likely to have occurred under the new Model GPWT designation, with special notations in the model possibly to denote the narrower tread. That's exactly what happened with Deere's Decision 2875 of November 18, 1929, when the company called for the introduction of the General Purpose Wide Tread Series P tractor. This tractor would differ from the traditional GPWT much like the 68-inch version of the GP Tricycle had varied from the regular GP Tricycle. For instance, the GP Wide Tread Series P also featured a 68-inch rear tread, a feature that was made possible in part by making both the right and left axle quills shorter. Also, 44x8-inch rear steel wheels and 24x4-inch front steel wheels would be used on this model. The Decision further stated that both the power shaft and lift system would be standard equipment on this new model. Deere documents indicate that Decision 2875 was put into action on January 23, 1930, when the GPWT Series P number P5000 rolled off the line.

Even though the GPWT obviously provided considerable crop clearance beneath the tractor, including the rear axles, the full-width drawbar did at times inhibit crop clearance.

The GP Wide Tread Gets a Boost

When the GP Wide Tread started production, it used pretty much the same engine as that of the basic GP tractor. Both engines used a water injection system, but the system had some problems with plugging up. Deere decided to eliminate the water injection system on its GP Wide Tread first, but that move was anticipated to cause a drop in tractor horsepower. To make up for the difference, Deere decided to boost the bore of the Wide Tread's engine from 5-3/4 inches to 6 inches. This change first affected tractor 402040 in April 1930.

This change in the GP Wide Tread affected how the Series P tractors were produced. The earliest GP Wide Tread Series P tractors had been converted from GP Wide Tread tractors. However, that process ended with serial number P5149. After that, Deere converted regular GP standard-tread tractors to fill the need for the GPWT Series P. According to the Serial Number Registers at Deere Archives, the following GP Standards were converted into GPWT Series Ps, which Deere abbreviated as GPPs in the Register:

Potato-style front wheels could be obtained on the GPWT, which was one way for Deere to satisfy the needs of potato growers.

GP Standards Converted into GPWT Series Ps (GPPs)

GP 222283 changed to GPP 5182
GP 222384 changed to GPP 5180
GP 222391 changed to GPP 5150
GP 222393 changed to GPP 5153
GP 222398 changed to GPP 5151
GP 222401 changed to GPP 5154
GP 222407 changed to GPP 5152
GP 222408 changed to GPP 5188
GP 222411 changed to GPP 5155
GP 222413 changed to GPP 5177
GP 222419 changed to GPP 5181
GP 222420 changed to GPP 5178
GP 222422 changed to GPP 5176
GP 222423 changed to GPP 5187
GP 222431 changed to GPP 5186
GP 222438 changed to GPP 5190
GP 222505 changed to GPP 5157
GP 222577 changed to GPP 5164
GP 222587 changed to GPP 5171
GP 222593 changed to GPP 5165
GP 222604 changed to GPP 5189
GP 222610 changed to GPP 5184
GP 222612 changed to GPP 5185
GP 222627 changed to GPP 5162
GP 222638 changed to GPP 5199
GP 222641 changed to GPP 5183
GP 222644 changed to GPP 5166
GP 222646 changed to GPP 5179
GP 222647 changed to GPP 5161
GP 222649 changed to GPP 5168
GP 222652 changed to GPP 5167
GP 222654 changed to GPP 5159
GP 222661 changed to GPP 5198
GP 222665 changed to GPP 5196
GP 222672 changed to GPP 5200
GP 222674 changed to GPP 5193
GP 222681 changed to GPP 5202
GP 222685 changed to GPP 5163
GP 222688 changed to GPP 5195
GP 222691 changed to GPP 5197
GP 222700 changed to GPP 5160
GP 222702 changed to GPP 5201
GP 222713 changed to GPP 5194
GP 222746 changed to GPP 5192
GP 222767 changed to GPP 5191

Top: The GPWT Series P tractor was designed to satisfy the row requirements for potato cultivation. Earlier GP Tricycle tractors experimented with 68-inch rear tread, leading to this model.

Drop-box housings on the rear axles gave the GPWT, like the original GP, the advantage of additional crop clearance under the rear axles.

Inset above: The wheels on the GP Series tractors should all be painted John Deere yellow; the rear hubs should be green, however, like the majority of the rest of the tractor. A little rubbed-off paint in places, such as the tips of the wheel lugs or the clutch pulley brake surface, shouldn't be cringed at, these tractors were designed for use.

A 1931 model, this GPWT features both an exhaust stack and an air intake stack. The air intake stack should be entirely John Deere classic green, whereas the exhaust stack is appropriate being black.

GP Wide Tread Series P production ended with number 5202, which was produced on August 19, 1930. All numbers were used, meaning that a total of 203 GP Wide Tread Series Ps were produced in the nearly seven months that the model was in production. That count excludes the GP Tricycles that were converted to have 68-inch rear treads.

The GPWT had been using the new 6-inch-bore engine since April 1930, but it wasn't until August 1930 that the bigger bore was extended to the GP Standards as well. The first such tractor to receive the new 6x6-inch engine was GP 223803.

People often ascertain the identity of the solid front wheels of certain GPOs as a means to identify that model. The solid front wheels eliminated the possibility of limbs being caught in the front-wheel spokes.

If you want to be technical about tires on these tractors, make sure that you use tires with 45-degree lugs. The modern lug angle was not in use when these tractors were produced, but it is okay to restore your tractor using such tires if you can't find 45-degree treaded tires for a reasonable price. It won't be 100 percent correct, but what's most important is that these tractors are alive and running.

The Model GPO

Deere introduced its first true orchard tractor, a derivative of the Model GP, in late March 1931. The new model—designated the Model GPO—used the 6x6-inch engine that was used on all the GP Series variations by that time. This model differed from the rest, however, mainly in stature. Only 49 inches tall at the top of the radiator cap, the GPO was just over 5 inches shorter than the GP Standard. Also, the GPO was 9 inches longer than the GP Standard. The added length was necessary in part to lower the operator's position as was best for orchard work.

Like the original Model GP, the Model GPO orchard tractor came standard with basic fenders. Fuller citrus-type fenders could be ordered as additional equipment on the GPO.

The "JOHN DEERE" decals
should appear centered on the
side of the hoods of these
tractors. The application of these
decals is often easiest with the
stacks removed, as some of the
letters actually appear behind
the stacks.

No stacks? Unlike the other GP
models of its time, the GPO did
not feature any stacks of any
kind. Deere did this simply to
prevent the stacks from
interfering with the trees in
the orchard.

The GPO came standard with 42.75x10-inch rear steel wheels and 24x6-inch spoked front steel wheels. Cast front steel wheels were often ordered on these tractors, however. Another popular option for the GPO was the full citrus fenders. Other options included rubber tires and dual rear wheels. Deere also sent a handful of the GPO tractors to be fitted with the Lindeman track system by that Yakima, Washington, company; the exact number and serial numbers of those units are unknown, however.

Production of the GPO spanned just weeks over the four-year mark, ending in the spring of 1935. The serial numbers for this model started with 15000 and ended at 15732, meaning that this is one of the more collectible versions of the GP Series.

The GPWT Gets a New Look

During the 1932 model year, starting at serial number 404810, the GP Wide Tread underwent a variety of changes

The low-profile Model GPO is among the most highly sought-after GP Series models. Even more desirable are the ultrarare Lindeman versions of this model, fully equipped with the Lindeman track system.

Right: One of the ways the GP could deliver its power was through the belt pulley. That feature, along with the power lift and traditional drawbar of the unit, helped make the GP versatile.

Below: The late-Model GP tractors featured what is commonly called a "square" engine; that is, the bore and stroke of the engine were the same: 6 inches.

that gave the model an all-new look. These changes were largely outlined in Deere's Decision 4100 of December 21, 1931. The Decision indicates that most of the changes were done to improve operator visibility. For instance, Deere tapered the radiator, hood, and fuel tank toward the rear of the tractor in order to remove obstructions from the operator's line of vision. The tapering of the fuel tank caused its capacity to drop from 16 gallons to 14 gallons, but that reduction was apparently considered an acceptable sacrifice in order to improve visibility for the operator. Additionally, the operator's position was altered, moved forward 11.5 inches and upward 9.5 inches. The new position gave the operator a better overall view of the ground in almost all directions.

Perhaps the most noticeable modification to occur at this time was the change in the steering system of the tractor. Previously, the GPWT used a side steering system much like that used on the GP Standard tractors. At 404810, however, the GPWT received an over-the-top steering system. This necessitated the addition of a front pedestal at the very front of the tractor, just in front of the radiator. A steering gear topped the pedestal, and connected to it was the steering rod, which ran all the way back to the operator. The steering rod ran between the new exhaust and air intake stacks that were both positioned side by side and protruded through the radiator top tank. Another change that Decision 4100 called for was the lengthening of the front-end casting. This change moved the cultivator mounting positions forward by 6 inches, and it also resulted in a new longer wheelbase of 84-5/16 inches for the GPWT.

With all of the changes that the GPWT underwent at serial number 404810 in early 1932, the model looked

very similar to what would become the Model A John Deere, which would appear late in 1933. Indeed, the experimental models that preceded the Model A were in the works at this time, and the success of the new visibility-improving features of the GPWT undoubtedly had some influence on the design ideas implemented on those experimental models and the eventual regular-production Model A.

The End of the GP

With the arrival of the Model AR, the GP and GPO were no longer necessary in Deere's lineup. Thus, Deere issued Decision 5399 stating that GP and GPO production would be discontinued "when appox. 30 Orchard Tractors now in process are completed." According to accompanying Deere documents in Deere Archives, this decision was put into effect on GP 230745 on February 28, 1935, and on GPO number O 15732 on March 30, 1935.

As mounted implements become increasingly popular, collectors show their tractors fitted with the implements that allowed them to get the job done. Implements also help give tractors a little more character, as a GP with a planter setting next to a plain GP will usually catch more attention.

The Model A Series

Today the John Deere Model A is among the best-known tractors with collectors almost everywhere. While it did not enjoy a production run as impressively long as Deere's Model D, the A was in Deere's line for a full 20 years in various versions with eye-catching production numbers. More important, though, were the Model A's contributions to Deere and to agriculture in general.

The Model A is most famous for being one of the earliest row-crop tractors with adjustable rear tread. Beginning regular production in the 1934 model year, the basic row-crop A featured splined rear axle shafts, which made it possible to change the rear-wheel tread of the tractor. This feature alone made the A more adaptable to numerous different agricultural applications. As will be

Opposite: Whether being used in a pumpkin patch or any other bedded crop, the AWH was at home. One distinct advantage of this model—in addition to its high clearance—was that both its front and rear wheels could be positioned to run between the same rows.

The John Deere Model A is a very popular tractor with collectors today, and since it was available in a wide array of configurations and underwent volumes of changes, this model is one of the most challenging and fun to collect. Shown here are tractors representing each of the five years during which the row-crop A was produced in the unstyled state. The unstyled tractors are particularly sought after by collectors.

The A is most noted for being one of the earliest row-crop tractors in the 2-3 plow class to feature adjustable rear tread width.

Steel wheels came as standard equipment on the unstyled A row-crops, even though the style shown here—which was particularly useful in sandy conditions—is not very common. A variety of special wheel types were available to suit different needs.

that model's designation less oomph in distinguishing it as a row-crop–type tractor.

The GP Tricycle did have the two narrow-set front wheels and drop-box rear axles, making it look much like the rather successful Farmall that the International Harvester Corporation was producing. A relatively successful design, the GP Tricycle evolved into the GP Wide Tread. Despite the advantages of both the GP Standard and the GP Wide Tread, Deere was not fully satisfied, as both models had substantial limitations, though different from each other in many cases. If only Deere could combine the advantages of both designs into one tractor model (and eliminate the problem of fixed tread widths), the company would have a nearly perfect row-crop tractor.

As a result, Deere & Company started experimenting with those basic ideas in 1931, and the first substantial experimental model was the Model FX, which still bore a strong resemblance to the GPWT. The successor, the Model GX, looked much more like the eventual production Model A. Then, for 1933, Deere decided to produce 10 preproduction tractors to be designated the Model AAs, although only 8 were ever produced.

revealed later, Deere had more to be proud of in the Model A than just one feature alone.

The Precursors to the Model A

The Model A probably would never have come into being had it not been for the advances that Deere and the tractor industry in general had made up until that point. For well over a decade, tractor manufacturers had been attempting to design a very adaptable, effective, and efficient row-crop–type general-purpose tractor. Deere had been very active in that quest, as well.

The search for the ideal row-crop tractor configuration led many companies to produce tractors that were classified as all-purpose units. Deere had participated in that area, as well, bringing forth its Model C in the 1928 production year. The C, which had a limited production lasting only about one month, led to the Model GP. Although the original GP was an all-purpose tractor, it was not exactly what Deere was looking for, either. Thus, the company began experimenting with tricycle-type versions of that model, which first led to the Model GP Tricycle. With that, the all-purpose GP was eventually dubbed the GP Standard, giving

The Model AA came in two basic variations, the AA-1 and the AA-3. The AA-1 featured a four-speed transmission, while the AA-3 only possessed a three-speed. Originally, Deere thought that the choice of transmission types would be advantageous to sales of this model, but the three-speed AA-3 eventually stopped production altogether, as the AA-1 was deemed superior.

Beginning with serial number 410000 and ending with number 410007, the Model AA started the serial-number run that would eventually be used by the row-crop Model As. Deere then gave serial numbers 410008 to 410011 to four preproduction versions of the Model A, which saw production in March 1934.

Deere Introduces the Model A

Regular production of the unstyled Model A row-crop began in the 1934 model year at serial number 410012, with the first shipment of tractors occurring in April of that year.

From the start of production, these tractors boasted a horizontal, two-cylinder, 309-cubic-inch engine. This power-plant, which had a 5-1/2x6-1/2-inch bore and stroke, was designed to be operated using low-grade tractor fuels. That feature, along with the engine's efficiency of operation, was influential in giving the Model A a low operating cost, which was extremely important to farmers during the Great Depression and its aftermath. Indeed, Deere promoted this as the number one feature of this model for quite some time, with the better-known adjustability of rear tread width often coming in second on Deere's list of the A's advantages.

Another contributing factor to the wide acceptance and overall success of the Model A was its wide range of adaptability. Deere eventually offered the A in a number of variations, including the more common row-crop and standard-tread designs.

Starting in 1934, Deere subjected the Model A to a number of production changes, most of which were designed to improve field performance. These early modifications presaged a long history of production changes that would cause the Model A to flourish. Deere seemed to almost always make the right changes at the right times on the Model A, and as a result, it proved to be a very reliable tractor. Indeed, believe it or not, some Model A tractors, including a few unstyled examples, are still being used for actual farm labor to this day, while other units regularly participate in field activities at tractor shows and plow days.

The Unstyled A Models

From 1934 through part of 1949, various unstyled versions of the Model A were produced. The row-crop models received styled lines beginning in the 1939 model year, but the standard-tread versions remained unstyled until midway through 1949. Following is an explanation of the most notable changes that occurred to all of these unstyled tractors, along with an explanation of the advantages of the newly introduced versions, in chronological order.

By far the most popular version of the Model A was the basic row-crop type with two narrow-set front wheels. This style could be used for almost any kind of agricultural activity, though more specialized versions were better suited for certain crops.

The Model AR

Deere authorized production of the first major variation of the Model A with its Decision 5100 in January 1935. According to that Decision, the new model was to be of the standard-tread configuration and bear the designation Model AS. Actually, though, it became known as the Model AR (A Regular).

The standard-tread AR looked significantly different from its row-crop counterpart for obvious reasons. At first, Deere equipped the AR with 42-3/4x10-inch rear and 28x6-inch front steel wheels as standard equipment. The AR originally had a rear tread width that was fixed at 50-5/8 inches when fitted with the standard wheel equipment, but a tread width of 54-1/8 inches was attainable by reversing the rear wheels. (Late in 1935, however, Deere started installing all rear wheels on the AR in the "reverse" position as standard practice.) Its design made it well suited for wheat-growing regions, where the most common duties it would perform would be pulling a plow or powering belt-driven equipment.

In the beginning, the AR used the same engine as did the row-crop A's 309-cubic-inch engine with 5-1/2x6-1/2-inch bore and stroke. In the AR, that engine was initially rated at 975 rpm, just as in the row-crop A. The Model AR continued production in the unstyled state until the 1949 model year.

The Elimination of the Open Fan Shaft (Row-Crop A)

The most notable early change in the row-crop A was the elimination of the "open" fan shaft. This long engine-driven shaft powered the cooling fan for the radiator. Up until mid-1935, the A sported a fan shaft that was partially exposed starting just behind the water manifold. Making the model a little safer, Deere enclosed the entire fan shaft within a tube starting at serial number 414809.

The Model AO

Deere's Decision 5530 in late May 1935 announced a more specialized version of the standard-tread Model A. This model, the AO (A Orchard), was regularly equipped with turning brakes and a low air stack and muffler, all of which made the tractor very desirable for use in orchards. In most ways, the AO was very similar to the Model AR, having most of the same features and undergoing many of the same production alterations.

One notable aspect of Model AO history, however, was the lapse in production it encountered. Deere ceased production of the unstyled AO for the 1937 model year, which was when Deere began producing the sleeker Model AO-S (or AO Streamlined). AO-S production continued through the 1940 model year, and production of the basic unstyled Model AO resumed for the 1941 model year. Like the AR, the AO

continued to be produced in the unstyled state until the 1949 production year.

The Model AW

The first major row-crop variation to be introduced was the Model AW (A Wide), which Deere first made available in the summer of 1935. The AW was nearly identical to the basic row-crop A; the main difference was the AW's use of a wide adjustable front axle, which made this variation well suited for use in bedded crops. The AW had the advantage of only needing wheels positioned between two pairs of crop rows instead of three. Throughout its production, the AW underwent most of the same changes that the basic A experienced, as well.

The Model AN

In July 1935, Deere published its Decision 5640 announcing yet another variation of the basic row-crop A tractor. This new model, which featured a single 9.00x10-inch front tire, was designed for use in vegetable crops planted in rows of 28 inches or less. Deere designated this single-front-wheeled version the Model AN (A Narrow).

The Model AI Introduced: The Standard Becomes Industrialized

John Deere's Model AI (A Industrial), authorized by Decision 6100 of February 1936, was a very rugged tractor. Designed to stand up to the demands of industrial use, the AI featured a stronger front axle and a shorter wheelbase

The more specialized the Model A became, the better it could do certain activities. And, typically, the more specialized a version of the A is, the rarer it is, as well. Thus, collectors often try to seek out tractors such as this Model AW to make their collection more diversified.

than its agricultural counterpart, the Model AR. The shorter wheelbase not only made the AI quicker-turning, but also made it possible to place front-mounted industrial equipment closer to the radiator of the tractor, thus improving its stability and efficiency.

Deere only produced the AI in an unstyled form, with production terminating in the summer of 1941. The AI is noted for having a paint scheme that was much different from that found on the rest of the A variations. This tractor came standard from the factory painted Industrial Yellow with black lettering. Deere eventually made light red, gray, blue, orange, green, and a different yellow available as optional basic paint colors.

The Model AO Streamlined

The Model AO-S (or AO Streamlined) falls in the production years that are largely known for unstyled John Deere tractors. Even though the AO-S did not have the same curved lines that the later styled tractors are known for, it was still quite stylish.

The AO Streamlined saw production from 1937 to 1940, and it was very well suited for orchard work. It sported a wedge-shaped front grille and sweeping fenders and limb guards. Optional citrus fenders, which covered a large portion of the sides of the rear wheels and the tractor in general, gave the tractor unparalleled features for tree/fruit protection in orchards.

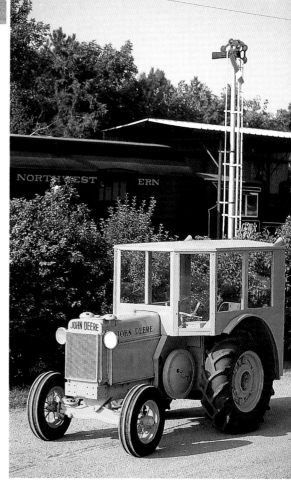

The AO-S featured a more compact design than did its predecessor Model AO, making it even better suited for orchard work. The AO Streamlined had a shorter wheelbase, which allowed it a tighter turning radius. Additionally, the tractor was closer to the ground and the operator sat at a lower position, both of which improved limb clearance. The sleek AO-S was narrower than the AO, as well.

The Model ANH

Deere's Decision 7253 from September 1937 authorized production of a high-clearance version of the Model A. The basis for the tractor was the Model AN, with the new variation being designated the Model ANH (A Narrow High). The high clearance of this model was attained by use of 9.00x40-inch rear tires, which increased crop clearance by about 2 inches. The clearance under the front end of the tractor increased 3-3/4 inches by the use of a narrower, but taller, 7.50x16-inch front tire.

The ANH also featured an increased rear tread adjustment range. Deere lengthened the rear-axle housings on this model by 2 inches and increased the total width of the rear axles from 82-1/2 to 98 inches. With those increases, tread widths from 56 to 80 inches were attainable with the wheels in the regular position. By reversing the wheels (which had their rims offset 6 inches from the center of their hubs), however, tread widths from 80 to 104 inches were also possible.

The Model AWH

Deere introduced its Model AWH (A Wide High) at about the same time the ANH appeared, being approved by Decision 7254 of October 1937. The AWH made use of the same 40-inch rear tires and extended rear axles and housings,

The Model AO-S has often been compared to a race car, although this model certainly did not boast high speeds. Its streamlined design was not intended for aerodynamics; it was for the protection of tree, fruit, and operator.

With its nose-up appearance, the ANH gave more clearance under both its front end and rear axles than did the basic Model AN. Today, the ANH is highly sought after by collectors, especially in the unstyled form.

Here we see a Model AWH and Model AW. Both tractors look strikingly similar, although the AWH is considerably rarer than the AW. Additionally, the AWH's 40-inch rear rubber tires are very difficult to find today without having to pay a fortune.

so the AWH and ANH were very similar. However, being based on the AW, the AWH also had an adjustable wide-front axle that provided the model with a front tread range with width adjustments from 42-5/8 to 54-5/8 inches. Special 7- and 13-inch front-axle extensions were also available, making front tread adjustments as wide as 66-5/8 and 80-5/8 inches possible, respectively. The AWH achieved its increased front-end clearance by using the same extended front-axle knees as those already being used on the somewhat smaller Model BWH (B Wide High) along with 5.50x16-inch front tires.

The Early-Styled A Row-Crops

Deere had big changes in store for its 1939 model year tractors, and the Model A was no exception. The row-crop As for that year had a brand-new look: they were styled!

The early-styled row-crop Model A tractors featured a sleek hood that flowed directly out of the contour of the

slatted-front grilles. These new grilles were the biggest contributing forces in giving the A a sleeker look, as they enclosed the radiator and concealed a portion of the front pedestal. The forward part of the front pedestal was the only portion of that component visible from the outside at first glance. It stuck out in front of the radiator grille screens by a few inches, and it stood higher at the center of its entire width. That shape ran all the way up the pedestal, with the steering gear being enclosed by a sheet-metal nose cone that had the same basic shape as the front of the pedestal. That shape, then pentagonal-like, extended all the way down the centerline of the hood as well, thus making this part of the tractor extend higher than the hood.

A common theme in Henry Dreyfuss' styling of the Model A was enhanced visibility for the operator. The sleek lines of the hood helped in that regard since it was also more wedgelike in shape when viewed from the top, with the narrowest portion being nearest the operator. Yet

The sun set on the production of the unstyled A row-crops with the start of the 1939 model year, as the new styled versions came on the scene. The unstyled row-crops may have had production limited to only five years, but they are still fairly easy to locate and make a nice addition to any collection.

effect hid the exhaust stack almost entirely from the operator's perspective.

Even though the changes already mentioned were significant and extensive, far more features were new to the 1939 row-crop As. These included, among others, an instrument panel, extended frame, improved seat, easier-to-reach controls, and a larger radiator.

The 1940 Changes

At the outset of the 1940 model A production (serial number 488000), Deere & Company made even more significant changes to the Model A.

The most noteworthy changes were made to the engine. Deere increased the stroke length by 1/4 inch to a total of 6-3/4 inches, which boosted engine displacement from about 309 cubic inches to about 321.2 cubic inches. Also new to this engine was its improved cylinder head, which was now of the "ramped" head design. This design produced better circulation within the cylinders, thus increasing the efficiency with which fuel was burned. The improved engine also made use of new connecting rods, pistons, and rings. Overall, these changes produced an increase in power, with the A now rating 26.36 belt horsepower at the University of Nebraska Tractor Tests.

The A received additional changes at that time, including alterations to the magneto, carburetor, final drives, rear axles, PTO, fuel tank, and radiator and shutters.

The early-styled A row-crops were immensely popular with farmers, and the model proved to be much more user-friendly than the unstyled units. They were very nice to look at, as well.

another notable characteristic of the styled A was the new location for the air intake and exhaust stacks. Instead of being placed on opposite sides of the tractor's hood, they were both placed within the centerline of the hood, with the exhaust stack forward. This meant that the operator's view was only obstructed by the air intake stack, since it in

Even though styled, these wartime Model As sit on steel wheels, an interesting contrast to the modernity of the tractor's general design. However, wartime demands for rubber in such items as aircraft tires seriously limited rubber supplies during World War II, so it is not at all unusual to find wartime As on steel.

The Model A During World War II

During World War II, the staggering rate with which changes were made to the Model A slowed significantly, but they still continued nevertheless. Additionally, rubber shortages during World War II forced many of these styled tractors to be produced and sold on steel wheels, even though rubber tires had become standard equipment by this time.

The Late-Styled A Row-Crops

As if making up for lost time, Deere & Company initiated a baffling number of changes on the Model A partway through the 1947 model year at serial number 584000, marking the beginning of the "late-styled" Model A production.

The quickest way to distinguish a late-styled A from an early-styled A is to look at the tractor's frame. Like the unstyled tractors, the early-styled As used a channel-iron–type frame, but the late-styled tractors used a new pressed-steel frame that more fully covered the engine.

At this point, electric starting became standard equipment on the A, thus allowing Deere to do a number of things to the A as standard practice. For instance, the starter was moved to an entirely new location, being placed in a housing located at the bottom of the crankcase. Thus, the starter engaged the flywheel at the bottom instead of at the top as it had done previously. Deere also chose to fully enclose the flywheel on these tractors, since none of the tractors would be of the hand-start type.

Since electric starting was now standard on these tractors, all tractors would be fitted with a battery. Deere killed two birds with one stone by applying a "battery-box" seat to the tractors. The new padded seat, which was adjustable forward and back to satisfy the operator's requirements, increased comfort. In addition, its support box provided a convenient location in which to store the battery. The presence of a battery-box seat on a Model A is another easy way to distinguish it as a late-styled model.

Another way to determine if an A is a late-styled model when viewing it from behind is to look at the rear-axle housings. For these tractors, the "JOHN" and "DEERE" lettering was removed from the left and right axle housings, respectively.

These new tractors also featured improved engines. Dubbed the "Cyclone" by Deere, this engine was available in two different fuel types. That option was entirely new to the A, as the model had been strictly an all-fuel-burning tractor from the start of production in 1934. But now, one style of the "Cyclone" was designed to burn low-grade fuels (just as all the earlier As had been designed), while the new version was engineered specifically to burn gasoline. On the whole, the "Cyclone" engines boasted even better circulation within the cylinders, plus longer pistons increased the compression ratio of the engine, even though it still retained the 5-1/2x6-3/4-inch bore and stroke.

Deere also changed the front pedestals on the A at this time, and in so doing, boosted the vertical clearance between

the front tires and the frame. Additionally, the Models AN and AW received special two-piece front pedestals that made it possible to interchange front axle types. Thus, a tractor that left the factory as a Model AN (narrow-front) could now appear to be a Model AW and no one would know the difference by just looking.

Yet another feature that Deere made available on the Model A at this time was the Roll-O-Matic front end. This special front-end assembly helped make operation of the A much smoother, especially in rough ground. It worked by a series of gears and knuckles that moved in order to raise one front wheel while lowering the other the exact same distance when needed. This feature cut the distance that the front end of the tractor moved up and down when encountering an uneven obstruction by exactly half the distance that it would have moved with the conventional rigid front-end assembly.

For the farmer, the late-styled As were amazing tractors, and one of the most important reasons why was the tractor's vastly improved hydraulic system. Deere called the new system the "Powr-Trol," and it provided the operator with a way to regulate the depth of mounted implements

In 1947, the Model AN totally took over the role that had previously been filled with the Model ANH. Deere accomplished that by giving the AN basically the same features that had been standard on the ANH up until that point. If farmers wanted, however, the old AN-type equipment could be fitted on these tractors on special order.

The late-styled tractors originally sported the decals in almost the same location as those found on the early-styled As, with the most notable exception being the late-styleds' use of the "A" in the circle decal on the grille sides. Sometime around the 1950 model year, however, the "JOHN DEERE" hood decals on these tractors were moved farther forward, being placed in the location seen on this tractor.

with just the move of a handle. The previous hydraulic system, the "Power Lift," was substantially limited in that it could only either raise implements all the way or lower them all the way. With the old system, that was done by simply kicking a lever at the operator's feet. Deere anticipated that the Powr-Trol would be widely accepted and in high demand, and the factories apparently experienced some difficulty producing enough units to meet demand. That is why Deere stated in its advertising literature as early as October 1946 that, "Insofar as production facilities will permit, the new Models 'A' and 'B' will be equipped with the Powr-Trol. Where Powr-Trol cannot be supplied, the regular hydraulic power lift will be furnished, and conversion assemblies will be made available at a later date if desired."

The late-styled Model As introduced other changes as well, including a new carburetor, 12-volt generator, voltage regulator, radiator, air cleaner, and drawbar assembly.

Important Changes in 1950

Two very important changes occurred to the A during the 1950 model year. The first was the use of the two-piece pedestal on all versions of the row-crop A, not just the AN and AW. The second was the incorporation of a gearshift quadrant much like the one that had been introduced on the Model B for 1947. This gearshift quadrant provided places for all six forward gears to be selected, instead of having to employ an overdrive lever to obtain certain gears.

The AH featured three different drawbar settings to accommodate the use of a variety of different implements. Deere even designed certain pieces of equipment specifically for use with this model.

The Model AH

Deere introduced the last major variation of the Model A during the 1950 model year. It was the Model AH (A Hi-crop). Often advertised as "The Famous Model 'A' *On Stilts*," the AH allowed 32 inches of crop clearance beneath the center of its rear axles. This was made possible by the use of special drop-box–type rear-axle housings.

The AH, which used a special high-clearance row-crop–type wide front axle with extra-long knees, had limited spacings that its front- and rear-wheel treads could be set at. For the rear wheels, 6-inch spacings were available, ranging from 60 to 90 inches. The front axle could also be set in 6-inch intervals, but they only ranged from 60 to 84 inches.

The Styled A Standard Treads

Deere finally styled its standard-tread versions of the Model A, now limited to the AR and AO, during the 1949 model year. These tractors bore a close resemblance to the newly introduced Model R, thus earning the Model AR the nickname of the "Baby R." The hood, grille, and exhaust and air intake stack arrangement closely resembled that of the R. The styled AR and AO may have looked a lot like the R, but they were actually quite different. Foremost was the fact that the R ran only on diesel, whereas the AR and AO burned either gasoline or all-fuel.

Today the Model A Series tractors are extremely popular with collectors, and their preservation is important in remembering our agricultural heritage. The A Series was one of the most revolutionary tractors of all time, its main claim to fame being the row-crop models' adjustable rear-wheel tread. But this model didn't stay so popular for so long without reason; indeed, the number of changes that the Model A underwent during its entire production is staggering, and the changes listed here are only the tip of the iceberg. For more detailed information about the history, changes, and originality issues regarding the Model A, Motorbooks' *Original John Deere Model A* is highly recommended.

Just like almost every other A Series tractor, the styled AR underwent many changes—so many, in fact, that one needs to be careful when trying to use one styled AR as a parts source in restoring another one.

The Model B Series

By early 1934, Deere & Company had in production two different sorts of tractors that together satisfied the needs of the two main categories of farming: wheatland-type grain work and row-crop work. The Model D was ideal for a variety of jobs in grain country, while the new Model A was specifically designed for use in row crops but could be used in just about any area of farming. Why could Deere have possibly wanted more?

The answer lies in the fact that, even in 1934, many farmers still had not taken advantage of the benefits of owning a tractor, meaning many tillers of the soil were still farming with horses for economical reasons. Throughout the early 1930s, the United States and most other countries of the world were suffering from the Great Depression. In the United States and Canada, farmers were struggling to survive, and the situation of many was worse in the Dust Bowl. Money was hard to come by, so many farmers didn't feel that they could afford to buy a new tractor. At the time, Deere's Model D had a base price tag of $1,050 while a Model A with no options cost $895. Those figures were simply too high for many farmers to feel financially comfortable in purchasing a tractor.

Just as Deere had wanted to find a way to start tapping the row-crop market via tractors back in the mid-1920s, the company wanted to tap additional segments of that same market in the mid-1930s. Deere felt the need to build a tractor that was larger than the A and would outperform an even greater number of horses, but the company realized that a tractor of that sort would cost more to produce and would therefore have a higher price tag. At the same time, Deere felt the need to have a tractor smaller than the A; that idea had two things that made it more attractive to the company. For one, Deere knew that a smaller tractor would ultimately cost customers less, thus making it more attractive to farmers. The other thing that spurred Deere toward the smaller end of the row-crop spectrum was the competition; for instance, the 1932 introduction of International Harvester's small Model F-12 had certainly caught Deere's attention.

The F-12 did, indeed, concern Deere & Company. Deere knew that International Harvester (IHC) was the sales leader in the tractor industry, with Deere following in

second place. Therefore, whatever IHC did to boost its sales potentially threatened to take away sales from Deere. Deere's soon-to-be Model A could run circles around the old Farmall Regulars, but IHC's larger Farmall F-30 was about 6 horsepower stronger than the A would be. Furthermore, the Farmall F-20, which IHC had introduced in 1932, was almost as powerful as the A would be on the belt, but the A could apply power to the ground better than the F-20 could. The A could compete with the larger F-30 if it had to, at least for a while, but Deere knew that IHC was sure to pull even further ahead of them in sales if Deere didn't try to compete with them in the smaller row-crop tractor market.

So, Deere decided to pursue the idea of a general-purpose row-crop tractor that was smaller than the Model A. The tractor would ultimately be approximately two-thirds the size of Deere's Model A, just big enough to compete with the F-12.

Opposite: For its horsepower class, the Model BO is a relatively narrow tractor. Overall, it was roughly only 50 inches wide, whereas the model was over twice that long.

Below: Introduced in the 1934 model year, the Model B John Deere became one of the most popular and versatile models in Deere's letter series. By production's end, the Model B had assumed more model variations than any other tractor in Deere's lineup. The most popular was the basic row-crop model seen here.

By September 1933, Deere had developed the experimental Model HX in its quest for a smaller general-purpose row-crop tractor. The tractor closely resembled the preproduction Model AA (which would become the production Model A) and looked much like the Model B would at its introduction. Since the HX was still an experimental tractor, though, Deere did not cast in the "JOHN DEERE" lettering in the radiator top tank as would be later done on the production As and Bs.

The Model HX had a few additional characteristics that set it apart from the upcoming Model B. First, the tractor used the cast steering-wheel hub that resembled a triangle with all three sides pushed in, much like the one used on the early Model A production units. Second, just as Deere left the "JOHN DEERE" lettering off of the radiator top tank on these units, those letters were also not present on the rear-axle housings as they would be during production.

Production Begins

The culmination of the Model HX experimentation came with Deere's issuing Decision 4600, announcing that the company would produce a new tractor model: the Model B. Deere assigned a new serial-number run to the new Model B, with production to begin at serial number 1000. That first tractor would not be completely assembled until October 2, 1934, a little later than the anticipated start date of the Model B production.

The Model B was, in most respects, exactly what Deere had envisioned: a scaled-down version of the Model A, a tractor that had been in production for approximately half a year before the B was released. At first glance, the B appeared much smaller than the A, but the differences in their specifications aren't all that big:

The Model B Versus The Model A

Model	B	A
Length	120.5 inches	130 inches
Width	85 inches	86 inches
Height	56 inches	61.5 inches
Wheelbase	80 inches	87.25 inches
Rear Tread	56–84 inches	56–84 inches
Weight	2,765 lbs.	3,700 lbs.

The earliest known variation of the Model B was the Model B Garden Tractor. This model, which would later be replaced by the Model BN, featured a single-front wheel and was ideal for cultivating vegetables and other specialized row crops.

Initially, the B received its power from a horizontal two-cylinder engine with a 4.25x5.25-inch bore and stroke. Compared to the Model A's specifications at that time—having a 5.50x6.50-inch bore and stroke—the B's bore was slightly over 77 percent as big as the A's, and its stroke was just under 81 percent as long as the A's. Clearly, those figures mean the B's engine was just over two-thirds the size of the A's.

The power of the B was visibly demonstrated at the Nebraska Tractor Tests. The B's testing spanned a rather large amount of time, but it wasn't the B's fault at all. Instead, it was the weather's, as conditions were not favorable for performing impartial testing on the B. Thus, even though Test 232 began on November 15, 1934, on the sixth Model B produced, that test did not conclude until April 19, 1935. The results rated the B at 14.3 brake horsepower. It delivered as much as 16.01 maximum load brake horsepower and 11.84 maximum load drawbar horsepower. With the results of the rated load tests, the B proved about 60 percent as powerful as the A.

Above: The Model B Garden Tractor made use of what is known as the four-bolt pedestal. Four-bolt pedestals feature only four bolts protruding from the front edge of the pedestal casting, and those four bolts attached the pedestal to the frame (also known as front-end support) of the tractor.

Top: This 1937 Model BW has both its front and rear wheels set far apart. The adaptability of this unit to various row and crop bed sizes made it popular with a variety of farmers of bedded and other specialized row crops.

In early 1935, Deere replaced the original four-bolt pedestal on the Model BN with an eight-bolt front pedestal as seen in this photo.

Next page: Collectors consider the BN John Deere a very desirable tractor. Even the eight-bolt version of this model is sought after, although most collectors prefer the four-bolt version.

As for how the B stood up against the Farmall F-12, it did quite well. The B was tested on distillate, while the F-12 endured two different tests. The first test of the F-12 was performed with the tractor operating on gasoline, and it yielded only slightly more horsepower than the B. However, when tested on kerosene—a fuel more comparable to distillate for its qualities—the F-12 was less powerful than Deere's new B.

The Model B Garden Tractor and The Model BN: The First Derivatives Appear

One thing for which the B is quite well known is the large number of its model variations. What some people aren't aware of is just how quickly those variations started appearing.

Deere first released a version of the B with a single-front wheel at serial number 1043, just 44 tractors into B production. All of the single-front-wheeled Model Bs produced during the 1934 model year are

Many people think that the Model B simply followed in the footsteps of its big brother, the Model A; however, that is not true. In fact, the first variation of the Model B was the BN, whereas the first variation of the Model A was the AW. And what's more, the second derivative of the Model B—the Model BW, such as the one seen here—even appeared before the first variation of the A Series.

generally known as Model B Garden Tractors, though these tractors are sometimes called Model BNs.

This BN, serial number 5731, is one of the "short frame" or "short hood" unstyled Bs. All row-crop Model B Series tractors prior to serial number 42134 featured a 44.5-inch frame. But, during the 1937 model year, these tractors received both longer frames and longer hoods, resulting in the "long frame" or "long hood" unstyled Model Bs.

the BN made use of the eight-bolt front pedestal.

In February 1935, beginning with tractor number 3043, the Model B received a new front pedestal. Originally, the Model B made use of a front pedestal that only had four bolts—two on each side—that attached it to the frame of the tractor. The new pedestal, however, made use of eight bolts—four on each side—to do the same job. Since this change occurred so early in Model B production, four-bolt Bs are highly sought after by collectors.

The Model BW Introduced

Tractors that are now known as Model BWs were approved for production by Decision 5252 of January 28, 1935. It is interesting to note, however, that that Decision never specifically called these new tractors Model BWs, simply referring to them as Model Bs with optional adjustable-tread front axles. That distinguishing feature gave these new tractors a 56- to 80-inch front tread width range. The company estimated that 20 wide-front Bs would be produced on steel wheels for the first year of production, while only 5 rubber-tired units were predicted for that

One of the many keys to success for the BW was its front spindles. These spindles allowed the front axle of the tractor to run horizontally out to the inside edges of the front wheels, where the spindles then dropped straight down to attach to the front wheel hubs. This gave the BW the crop clearance it needed under its front axle. The spindles on this tractor have been painted appropriately.

Indeed, even the coding in the Serial Number Registers in Deere & Company Archives indicate that the last three 1934 Model Bs—bearing serial numbers 1800, 1801, and 1802—were Model BNs. Like the later Model BNs, the Garden Tractors featured a front yoke with a single-front wheel instead of the conventional narrow-set, two-wheeled assembly used on the basic B. Like all of the earlier Model Bs, the Garden Tractors made use of a four-bolt–type front pedestal. And, like all of the later Model Bs,

From the older generation to Deere's "New Generation" Series today, John Deere tractors have long been known for their reliability and operator conveniences. Over time, so did the number and quality of those conveniences, helping make John Deere tractors as successful and popular.

For the row-crop versions of the Model B, fenders were almost always an option, but many farmers found them unnecessary. When Deere unveiled the standard-tread versions of the Model B, however, the company decided that fenders should be standard equipment for those models.

year. The first Model BW was B 4479, which Deere produced in April 1935.

Special Rear Axles

Decision 5489 of May 13, 1935, approved the use of special optional 84-inch rear axles on anywhere from 45 to 50 Model Bs. An accompanying document indicates that feature adorned the following 50 tractors starting in mid-July 1935:

Model Bs Fitted with 84-inch Rear Axles

8099 to 8110
8789 to 8795
8797 to 8808
9366
9368
9373 to 9377
9379
9382 to 9384
9388 to 9390
9392
9402
9403
9407
9545

Interestingly, though, Deere & Company's Model B Serial Number Registers only note the 84-inch axle on tractors 8099 to 8110, 8791, 8792, 8797, 8798, 8800, 8801, and 8805 to 8808. Deere shipped most of those tractors to Arizona.

The Model BR: The First Standard-Tread B

With Decision 5600 of July 24, 1935, Deere made known its decision to produce the Model BR tractor—a tractor that was intended "[t]o meet the field requirements for a smaller, lighter, and less powerful standard tread tractor than the Model 'AR'."

At first glance, one may be tempted to say that this tractor must be a Model BR since it does not have full citrus/orchard fenders, which cover the rear wheels on many BOs. But, in all actuality, the standard fenders on the BO were much like those of the BR, and the full citrus fenders were merely an option for the BO, not standard equipment as a number of people believe.

Deere produced the Model BR with a 553-rpm PTO shaft installed as standard equipment. The BR also used a four-speed, 1:2.05 overdrive transmission, which provided speeds between almost 2 miles per hour and 6-1/4 miles per hour.

To comply with the design of a standard-tread tractor, the BR had shorter rear-axle housings than the basic row-crop B, thus allowing a tread of 44-1/4 inches with the standard 40x8-inch rear steel wheels in the normal position. Even though the rear-wheel tread was not adjustable by moving the rear wheels on the axles as was the case with the row-crops, the rear-wheel tread on the BR could be changed by reversing the rear wheels, resulting in a 3-inch narrower rear tread. The BR used a fixed-tread front axle onto which 24x5-inch front steel wheels were mounted. Since the design of the BR was so drastically different from the row-crop B, Deere opted to give the model its own serial-number run. The first BR—serial number 325000—rolled off the line on September 16, 1935.

Deere designed the Model BO to have a low profile with as few obstructions as possible. Thus, the air intake stack was eliminated on this model, and replaced by a rounded-off air intake opening guard. Similar guards were installed ahead of the fuel-tank caps so that the stacks would be less likely to catch tree branches.

Left: Like the Model AR, the new Model BR featured a fixed, standard, or "regularized" rear tread width. This version was introduced for farmers who wanted a tractor of the more traditional design, a design such as that of the venerable John Deere Model D, which was ideal for pulling implements and powering belt-driven equipment. The Model BR couldn't do anything else that the general-purpose B could do, but some would argue that what the BR could do, it did better than the basic B.

The full citrus fenders were a very popular option on the Model BO, and for good reason. With that feature, the possibility of damaging trees in orchards was much diminished, as the full fenders helped lift tree limbs over the tractor's tires.

The Model BO Appears

Only 85 tractors after the BR started production, Deere further specialized the unit. A new model, the BO orchard tractor, shared the same serial-number run with the BR, since Deere based both models on the same chassis design. The new BO, adopted by Decision 5701 of September 11, 1935, was different from the BR primarily in having differential brakes that provided a shorter turning radius, a lowered air stack, and shields for the air stack and fuel caps. The first BO—which rolled off the line on September 26, 1935—bore serial number 325084.

A Model BO would make a wonderful addition to almost any collection, especially if restored with meticulous attention to detail. The outside of these tractors is important, indeed, but the true success and heart of the model lie in its internal workings.

Hello yellow. The Model BI usually painted yellow, not green, but this tractor is John Deere through and through despite not being John Deere green. The yellow paint scheme was required or preferred on this tractor to make it more visible when performing industrial duties.

Below: Deere & Company designed its B Series tractors, including the Model BI, to be able to run well on low-cost, low-grade fuels. This was important for all applications at the time this tractor was produced, because of the Great Depression.

The Model BI Introduced

An industrial version of the Model B, denoted the Model BI, appeared starting with tractor 326016 in late March 1936. The result of Decision 6150, the Model BI sported Highway Yellow paint with black stenciling, just like the AI. Similarly, the BI featured machine-surfaced finished pads with tapped holes in the front-end casting, a feature that made attaching front-mounted industrial implements possible. To allow those front-mounted units to be placed closer to the radiator, Deere moved the front axle of the BI back 5-1/4 inches from the location on the BR. This reduced the tractor's wheelbase from 68 inches (the wheelbase of the Model BR) to only 62-3/4 inches. With the shorter wheelbase, the

BI also had a tighter turning radius than the Model BR. The BI had an 11-foot, 3-inch turning radius, whereas the BR's turning radius was 5 inches greater.

Unlike the other standard-tread Bs, the BI came standard with rubber tires. Deere installed 9.00x28-inch low-pressure rear tires on the BI as standard equipment, and the model also came standard with 5.50x16-inch low-pressure front tires. The Model BI also featured a cushioned seat and backrest that could be adjusted forward or backward over a range of 3 inches.

On June 29, 1937, Deere issued Decision 7129 approving the use of a variety of special colors (in addition to the

Yellow wasn't the only color that John Deere painted its industrial BI. Special orders could be requested for colors other than yellow or John Deere green, and red was one of them. Note that this red BI features black trim and lettering, just as is the case with the yellow BIs.

Right: The downswept exhaust pipe was popular on the Model BI, because in that position the exhaust was less likely to asphyxiate the operator. Both the color of the exhaust and the magneto on this tractor are appropriate.

Far right: Radiator shutters were used on these tractors to help regulate engine-operating temperature. The shutters can be seen inside the radiator grille screen, and the shutter control is evident on the left just below the radiator top tank.

A bird's-eye view of this red BI reveals both the oval, cast-iron radiator cap and the special seat that is found only on the industrials. The padded seat made operating these tractors in sometimes-rigorous industrial applications a little more comfortable for the operator.

The Model BI was shorter-coupled than the Models BR and BO, made possible by having its front axle placed 5-3/4 inches farther back. This proved advantageous for industrial applications.

standard Industrial Yellow with black lettering) for all of Deere's industrial tractors. The special colors included light red, gray, blue, orange, green, and even other shades of yellow. While Deere probably painted most BIs Industrial Yellow, at least one BI is known to have been painted red from the factory.

The Model B Lindeman Crawlers

For some time, the Lindeman Power Equipment Company of Yakima, Washington, converted a variety of Model B Series tractors—including BOs, BRs, and even one BI—into crawler-type tractors. Various estimates exist as to how many such units were made, but all estimates seem to indicate

The John Deere BO Lindeman crawler is the most well known of the Model B Series Lindeman crawlers. Approximately 1,700 such units saw production, whereas only a handful of BR Lindeman crawlers and only one known BI Lindeman crawler were ever made.

somewhere around 1,700. Deere shipped the tractors that were to be converted into crawlers to Lindeman, and oftentimes the tractors were shipped without wheel and tire equipment, since those components weren't going to be necessary once the tractors were placed on track systems. Once Lindeman received the units, the company added the track system, steering clutches, final drives, and other related components necessary to make full-fledged crawler tractors out of standard-tread Bs.

When production of the Model B Series Lindeman Crawlers started is not clear at all. The records on this are fuzzy, and the most reliable seem to be the Serial Number Registers at Deere & Company Archives. They at least give us an idea of when the first BO tractors were shipped to Yakima, Washington, and when shipments were made expressly to the Lindeman Power Equipment Company itself.

The earliest BOs that the author found as being shipped to Yakima were serial numbers 332211 to 332220, but the earliest BOs that the author found that the Serial Number Registers indicated were shipped directly to Lindeman were serial numbers 332901 to 332907. The end of John Deere B Series Lindeman production seems to have occurred with serial numbers 337336 to 337345, since that is the last batch of tractors that the author found in the Serial Number Registers of Deere & Company as having been shipped specifically to Lindeman.

The Serial Number Registers also reveal other information about the shipment of the BO, BR, and the one BI tractor to Lindeman. The earliest tractors seem to have all been fitted with citrus fenders, 24x5-inch front steel wheels with 12 spokes, and 40x8-inch rear steel wheels with 10 spokes. However, starting with the shipment of tractors

The John Deere–Lindeman crawlers came about as a result of the cooperation of Deere & Company and the Lindeman Power Equipment Company of Yakima, Washington. Deere shipped engines, transmissions, rear ends, and other related parts for their standard-tread B Series tractors to Lindeman, where Lindeman fitted the wheelless tractors with track assemblies, turning clutches, and the like.

334381 to 334385, almost all tractors were listed in the Serial Number Registers as being shipped with "finish assembly for Lindeman with differential drive gears."

The majority of the B Series tractors shipped to Lindeman were BOs. In fact, the author only found a handful of Model BRs that were shipped to Lindeman. Their serial numbers are as follow:

Model BRs Shipped to the Lindeman Power Equipment Company

333379	336513 to 336522
333381 to 333383	336524 to 336525
334370	336527
335351 to 335360	336744

The only Model BI known to have been shipped to Lindeman is number 330986, which is quite possibly the earliest B Series Lindeman crawler, and certainly the rarest.

The Model BW-40 Introduced

Decision 6731 announced that special equipment would be made available for the Model BW to narrow the tractor so that it could cultivate special crops produced mainly in California. By using shorter rear axles and housings, these specially designed Model BWs could have rear-wheel treads as narrow as 40 inches when fitted with steel wheels. Thus, even though these tractors seem to have never been specifically designated Model BW-40s by Deere, that is what they are known as by collectors today. A variety of other special components were necessary to make these tractors so narrow, but their production was ultimately extremely limited. Decision 7252 called for the discontinuance of the special equipment necessary to make these narrowed BWs, and it revealed that only six such tractors were ever produced. They were serial numbers 25150, 25173, 26271, 26965, 27097, and 27268, and Decision 7252 indicates that all six of those tractors were built using parts bearing experimental numbers.

The Model B Is Lengthened

Prior to June 1937, the frame of the Model A was longer than that of the Model B, meaning that both models had to use different frame-mounted implements. In order to make it possible for both models to be fitted with the same implements, Deere lengthened the frame of the Model B by 5 inches to 49.5 inches in June 1937. The last B to use what became known as the "short" frame (44.5-inch) was serial number 42133. Deere scrapped serial numbers 42134 to 42199 so that production of the long-framed Model B would start at an even serial number, 42200.

The High-Clearance Versions of the Model B

In two consecutively numbered Decisions, Deere brought to light two new models that were based on the Models BN and BW. Both of the new tractor models would sport items that gave them increased crop clearance. Thus, the new models were the BNH and BWH, the "H" signifying "High-Clearance." Soon thereafter, Deere would also introduce a special high-clearance B derivative with a narrow tread, the BWH-40.

The BNH

The BNH resulted from Decision 7250 of August 25, 1937. Designed for use in vegetable crops, this model featured rear-axle housings that were 2-7/8 inches longer than the regular B row-crops. This, coupled with special rear wheels that had the hubs offset from the centers of the rims by 6 inches, gave the tractor an impressive rear tread range of 56 to 104 inches. Tread widths of 80 to 104 inches were obtainable by reversing the rear wheels. Decision 7250 explained that, with those features, "row spacings from 14 to 26

At first glance, this tractor appears to simply be a Model BN. However, upon closer inspection, we see that this is instead the rarer model BNH. It has the longer rear-axle housings, thicker rear axles, and special rear wheels that gave the tractor added clearance under the rear-axle housings.

[inches] can be cultivated with four rows under the tractor, and spacings from 28 to 52 [inches] can be cultivated with two rows under the tractor." Since the BNH had such a wide rear tread, Deere opted to increase the diameter of the rear axles by 1/8 inch to increase their strength. The first BNH, produced on October 1, 1937, was tractor 46175 according to Deere documents. The final unstyled BNH was serial number 58176, built on June 8, 1938. In all, Deere produced only 66 unstyled BNH tractors, making this model highly collectible and highly sought after.

The BWH

October 1, 1937, marked the day that Decision 7251 announced the new Model BWH. Similar to the BNH in how the high-clearance aspects of the models were acquired, the BWH would come standard with 7.50x40-inch rear rubber tires. Those taller rear wheels added 2 inches of crop clearance under the rear axles, while 3 inches of clearance were added under the front axle by the extended front axle knees. The BWH also benefited from the longer rear-axle housings, providing this model with the 56- to 104-inch rear

Like the Model BNH, the BWH used longer rear-axle housings than the basic Model B. However, those housings still retained the "JOHN" and "DEERE" lettering just as on the basic B. The BNH and BWH were eliminated from Deere's lineup at the same time that the company dropped the lettering from those rear-axle housings, meaning that the BNH and BWH always featured that lettering. The face of these letters should be painted John Deere yellow on all the B Series tractors, which featured them.

tread adjustments. A front tread of 42 to 54 inches came from the standard-issue front axle on the BWH, but optional 7-inch and 13-inch extensions for the front axles could boost the front tread to 80 inches wide, respectively. B51679 was the first BWH, and was manufactured on December 15, 1937. Production of this rare model terminated on the same day that BNH production ended—June 8, 1938. The final BWH, serial number 58095, was the 51st such unit, making this model even rarer than its narrow-front counterpart.

The BWH-40

Decision 7252 of October 15, 1937, did not just put an end to the tractors that are now known as Model BW-40s. It also called for the use of special equipment to narrow the Model BWH in much the same manner as with the

BW. The Decision, which does not refer to these tractors as Model BWH-40s (the name given to them by collectors today), simply calls these tractors BWHs with special equipment, and it stated that 50 units were estimated for 1938 production. These tractors, like the BW-40s, came standard with fenders and made use of special shortened rear axles and housings. This arrangement provided rear tread widths of 42 to 80 inches with rubber tires. The tread range of 42 to 56 inches was possible with the rear wheels (which had the rims offset from the centers) having their rims set inward, and the range of 58.75 to 80 inches was possible by having the rims set outward. Deere documents indicate that the first such tractor was produced on December 15, 1937, bearing serial number 51679. Deere's estimated number of these tractors was a bit high, as only a dozen BWH-40s were produced.

When viewed alone, it may be difficult to distinguish a Model BWH from a BWH-40. However, when viewed alongside a BWH-40, this tractor is clearly a BWH, due to its wider stance.

The BWH-40 used special equipment like that used on the half-dozen BW-40s that Deere previously produced, features that made this model have a narrower stance than the basic BWH tractors. Despite their differences, however, the BWH and BWH-40 share the same basic paint schemes and decal placements that the basic Model B row-crops used; the only exception was the model designation stencil on the seat support channel.

The Early-Styled Row-Crop Model Bs

The Model B was the earliest of Deere's tractors to be subjected to the stylistic ideas of industrial designers Henry Dreyfuss and Associates. Along with the styling, however, Deere intended to improve the B mechanically. All of these changes were outlined in Decision 7600 of May 14, 1938, which stated that, "To improve performance of the Model B Series Tractors, we [the company] will replace present 4-1/4 x 5-1/4 engine with 4-1/2 x 5-1/2 engine, maintaining present speed of 1150 R.P.M. This will increase engine displacement 17%." These changes would require further modifications to the cooling system, air cleaner, and other such tractor components.

The first of the styled row-crop Bs was serial number 60000, produced on June 16, 1938, which kicked off the 1939 model year for that tractor. The standard-tread versions of

The profile of the styled Model B allows us to see both the intake and exhaust stacks, whereas with the unstyled Model B it was difficult to see one or the other of those stacks when viewing the tractor from the sides, as the stacks were originally side by side on the hood.

the B, however, did not receive the styled lines. They did benefit from the increased engine size and other such mechanical features beginning with serial number 329000 on June 15, 1938. Production of the styled row-crop Model B Series tractors included the basic Model B and the Models BN, BW, BNH, BWH, and BWH-40.

From September 6 to September 16, 1940, Model B number 60003 underwent testing at the University of Nebraska in Test 305. The B performed well in the tests, delivering good ratings while being tested with both spade steel wheels and rubber tires. On steel, the tractor produced 10.84 rated horsepower and 14.03 operating maximum load horsepower on the drawbar, up from the 9.38 and 11.84 numbers shown in the tests performed on the model four years earlier. On rubber, the B was even more effective in the drawbar tests, cranking out an impressive 16.44 horsepower under maximum operating load. As for brake horsepower, the B topped its previous ratings by over 2 horsepower, touting 16.94 rated and 18.53 maximum load horsepower.

Despite the stylizing of the row-crop versions of the Model B, Deere did not extend the styling to the standard-tread

Henry Dreyfuss & Associates first experimented with styled lines on the Model B. The most striking results of their work can be seen when viewing the sheet metal of a styled Model B.

Opposite top: The styling of the Model B didn't affect just the basic row-crop model—it affected all of the B series row-crop tractors. Here we see an unstyled and a styled Model BWH, both of which feature the same adaptations for wide front ends and high crop clearance.

Opposite bottom: When styling the basic Model B, Deere didn't just style the sheet metal on the tractors; indeed, even the front pedestal was streamlined. And, for the BWH, that streamlining on the front pedestal extended all the way down, even to the part where the pedestal attaches to the front axle.

Right: This close-up view of the front axle on the unstyled Model BWH-40 shows that the bolts that attached the front end to the frame of the tractor were originally exposed.

Below: As was the case with the BWH, the BWH-40s also received the benefits of styled lines. Note the differences in the markings on these tractors as well as the differences in the positioning of their intake and exhaust stacks.

Above: The styled Model BWH-40 underwent production only from 1939 to early 1947. Along with the BWH and BNH, the BWH-40 was eliminated from the line when Deere introduced the late-styled Model B row-crops. Thus, there were no pressed-steel framed BWH-40s produced.

Right: When Deere styled the front end of this model, the company repositioned the bolts attaching the front end to the inside of the frame, behind the front end. Thus, only the implement attaching bolts could be seen when viewing the tractor casually from the outside.

Roughly a dozen styled BWH-40s rolled out of the factory from 1939 to 1947. Thus, Deere produced only an average of just over one such tractor in each of those nine years. However, it is unclear if any BWH-40s underwent production during or after the years of 1942 to 1945 when wartime tractor production slowed significantly and tractors became harder for farmers to acquire.

Even though the row-crop Model B tractors received styling in 1939, the standard-tread versions of the B never received styled lines and were totally discontinued in the 1947 model year. Consequently, none of the B Series Lindeman crawlers were styled.

This 1947 Model BO Lindeman crawler bears serial number 337336, meaning that this tractor represents the beginning of the end for the B Series Lindeman crawlers. Tractor 337336 was the first serial number in the last batch of tractors (totaling 10 units) that Deere sent to Lindeman to receive the crawler conversion.

versions of the B at any point. Deere did give the BR and BO bigger engines, however, increasing their bore size to 4.5 inches. The BR and BO continued production for several more years in their unstyled form, but they still proved to be fairly popular with owners.

A Boost in Row-Crop B Power, Plus a New Tranny

On August 28, 1940, B96000 was the first Model B tractor to benefit from yet another boost in power. With its Decision 9100 of March 26, 1940, Deere called for a higher compression ratio, an improved combustion chamber, a new manifold and carburetor, and an improved cooling system for the Model B. The engine size and rated rpm stayed the same, however. It is important to note that the B also received a new transmission at this time; the original four-speed transmission was replaced with a six-speed unit. The six speeds could be attained by three gearshift lever positions when coupled with high- and low-speed ranges as available via the high-low shifter lever atop the transmission case.

It would be some time before the official horsepower numbers would show how effective these changes had been in boosting the horsepower of the Model B, but that wasn't

Deere's or the Model B's fault. Instead, the weather was to blame. Test 366 started on November 4, 1940, but unfavorable weather delayed completion of the test until April 25, 1941. Even though standard equipment on the Model B by that time included 10x38-inch rear tires with cast-iron centers, Deere decided to have the B tested using the optional, smaller 9x38-inch rear tires, as well. With that equipment, the B posted already impressive numbers, including 16.48 drawbar horsepower under maximum operating load. However, with the standard-equipment 10x38-inch rear wheels, the B pounded out 17.13 drawbar horsepower. The brake horsepower tests as performed on the Model B at this time proved that the tractor could deliver as much as 19.69 horsepower under maximum operating load on the belt.

Deere announced with Decision 12700 of May 1947 that the Models BR and BO were to be discontinued. This Decision, apparently retroactive, stated that this was to be effective on January 1, 1947.

The Late-Styled Model Bs Are Introduced

Deere updated the styling on the Model B in the 1947 model year at serial number 201000 on February 6, 1947. The new tractors had a variety of new features. The new features were similar to those made to the Model A at about the same time, including a new pressed-steel frame, the advent of electric starting as standard equipment, the enclosed flywheel, the new battery-box seat, the more futuristic-looking steering shaft support column, and more.

Not only were the cosmetic features of the B improved at this time, so were many mechanical characteristics of the unit. First, the Model B also made use of a new six-speed transmission that provided forward speeds of 1.5, 2.5, 3.5, 4.5, 5.75, and 10 miles per hour. The 1.5-mile-per-hour first gear speed was the slowest provided on the B to date; it was added in order to make the B more effective while doing close cultivation, transplanting, and other such jobs that required slow speeds. In addition to the six-speed transmission, the B

This early-styled Model B features optional fenders. Note the correct placement of the nose cone, hood, and clutch pulley stencils on this model, as well as its appropriate paint scheme.

When viewing both an early-styled and a late-styled Model B from a distance, people usually first notice the differences in the front-end support (frame) of the tractors. However, when sitting in the operator's seat, people always notice the late-styled's very different, far more comfortable padded seat with backrest.

Since there were no pressed-steel framed BWH-40s produced, just as there were no pressed-steel framed BWHs or BNHs, the model never came standard with electric starting. However, that was always an option on the model.

also benefited from a new gearshift quadrant. The new quadrant featured seven slots, one for each of the six forward gears and one for reverse, thus eliminating the need for the high-low shifter lever. Strangely enough, the B was the first tractor to receive such a gear quadrant, as the Model A would not receive that feature until the following year.

A second change benefiting the B from serial number 201000 was a bigger, more powerful engine. The bore of the engine was increased by 3/16 inches to 4-11/16 inches, giving the B's engine about 190 cubic inches of displacement, up about 15 cubic inches from the previous design. Additionally, Deere improved the turbulence within the cylinders of the engine, thus improving fuel combustion and increasing fuel economy. Deere dubbed these engines "Cyclone Engines," mainly for that noteworthy characteristic. Additionally, the new Cyclone engines were available in two different types: one was specifically designed as an all-fuel version (as almost all Deere tractors had been designed for

up to that point), whereas the second was designed specifically to burn gasoline, a fuel that was becoming more popular with farmers.

Still other features that the late-styled Model B could boast about were the new standard-equipment Powr-Trol hydraulic lift system and the optional Roll-O-Matic front-end assembly. The Powr-Trol's main advantage was that it provided specific depth control in raising and lowering implements, allowing for implements to be held at any position between all the way up and all the way down. The previous system—the Power Lift system—only allowed implements to be raised all the way up or all the way down; with it, there was no middle ground. The other new feature, the Roll-O-Matic front end, made running a tractor over rough, uneven ground much smoother, as both front wheels could move up and down in equal amounts to reduce the up-and-down movement of the front end of the tractor by half.

Elimination of the BNH and BWH

In order to cut down on the number of model variations available in the B series, Deere decided to drop the Models BNH and BWH from the line. This coincided with the appearance of the late-styled Model B at serial number 201000. However, so that the advantages of the Models BNH and BWH would not be lost, those features were then made standard equipment on the Models BN and BW. Thus, the new Model BN and BW tractors could be fitted with either 42-inch rear tires (which had been standard on the BNH and BWH) or with the 38-inch tires that the BN and BW had been fitted with before. When the 42-inch tires were chosen, the BN made use of a 6.50x16-inch front tire, and the BW made use of longer front-axle knees. Similar changes were also made with the Models AN and AW at this time, as Deere chose to eliminate the Models ANH and AWH from the line.

Interchangeable Front Ends for BN and BW

The Models BN and BW also made use of new interchangeable front ends. This consisted of two pieces, one being the top part that attached to the frame and extended up to the steering gear, and the other being the front yoke or the wide-adjustable front-axle assembly. This advantage would be extended to the regular Model B later in production.

The End of Production

The last of the Model B Series tractors to be produced was a basic Model B. Produced on June 2, 1952, that tractor—an all-fuel version—bore serial number 310772. Deere scrapped the remaining Model B serial-number plates, which ranged from numbers 310773 to 313999. But the legacy of the Model B would not end, as another model would soon replace it. That tractor, the Model 50, was a direct descendant of the highly successful Model B.

The Model G Series

By the time the Model A appeared in regular production in the spring of 1934, Deere already had a smaller tractor designated the Model HX in development, a project that ultimately led to the introduction of the Model B in the 1935 model year. Even before the B was on the market, however, Deere also recognized the need for a row-crop tractor that was *bigger* than the A. Thus, experimentation on a larger model, based on the design used by the Model A and the soon-to-be Model B, began late in 1934.

Deere's experimental model for this purpose was the Model KX. Unfortunately, records of the experimentation on this unit are very scarce, and it is unclear as to even how many Deere built. What is known, though, is that Deere originally intended to call the actual production tractor that would result from the KX the Model F. This made perfect sense since, by this time, Deere already had produced units including the Model A tractor, the Model B tractor, the Model C tractor, the Model D tractor, and the Model E engine. To introduce

a Model F next would make good sense when looking at it that way. But, when one considered the fact that International Harvester's row-crop series tractors were its F Series, having a Deere row-crop tractor designated Model F probably wouldn't have been a good idea. Thus, Deere changed its mind, opting for the next letter in the alphabet as this tractor's ultimate designation.

In the end, that made perfect sense, too: "G" sounds a lot like "D," and Deere's D had already firmly established itself as a rugged, dependable tractor. Also, the G was to have horsepower similar to that of the D. Thus, it only makes sense that those two models had similar-sounding designations.

The G Growls to Life

Deere approved regular production of the Model G in its Decision 6650 of January 16, 1937. This Decision read very much like the one that approved production of the

Opposite: Throughout its production, the Model G's frame bowed out just in front of the engine, as the large engine size was too big to fit the frame without alterations. The G featured an impressive bore and stroke of 6-1/2x7 inches, providing over 412 cubic inches of displacement.

When Deere first introduced the Model G, the model's steering shaft cleared the top of an un-notched radiator top tank. However, as those "low radiator Gs" experienced some field problems with overheating in the hot summers of the south, a new, bigger radiator had to be used. This made it necessary to add a notch in the radiator top tank so that the steering shaft would have the clearance it needed to operate.

The Model G John Deere entered Deere's line as the biggest tractor in the company's row-crop tractor line. The G roared into the Nebraska Tractor Tests in November 1937 to produce an impressive maximum PTO horsepower of 35.91 and maximum drawbar horsepower of 27.63. Those ratings put the G in contention with Deere's Model D for the most horsepower in Deere's line, though the D had the edge with a 1/4-inch-larger bore.

Model AA experimental tractors that led to the Model A. For instance, both documents touted the units' low manufacturing and operating costs, adjustability of tread, provisions for attaching implements, and improved field performance. With regard to the latter item, both tractors featured a high-horsepower-to-weight ratio that provided the drawbar with a greater percentage of applied power. Additionally, both tractors were lightweight in design, had large-diameter rear tires, and had proper weight distribution, all of which contributed to making operation of the tractors less taxing. The new G would also make use of the time-proven four-speed transmission, although one major difference between the G and the A was that the G used an underdrive transmission, as opposed to the A's overdrive transmission. In

addition, Decision 6650 announced that the G would be regularly equipped with a power shaft (PTO) from the start of production. The G was designed for use in crops with row spacings from 30 to 42 inches or in rows of 20 inches of less, as it had a rear-wheel tread of 60 to 84 inches.

The Model G began production powered by a big horizontal, two-cylinder engine with a 6-1/8x7-inch bore and stroke. The first Nebraska Tests administered on this model revealed its 20.75-rated drawbar horsepower and its 31.51-rated and 35.91-maximum-load-belt horsepowers. The G also mustered 20.75-rated drawbar horsepower and 27.63-maximum-load drawbar horsepower. These tests were performed on G number 1081 in November 1937. Interestingly, the G ended production using the same-sized engine that it started out with, though many improvements had been made to it in that time.

The serial-number run for the Model G began with 1000. However, the first two tractors were listed as experimentals. Tractor 1000 underwent a variety of experiments, and was later retagged serial number 2810. G1001, however, was later scrapped. Serial number 1002, produced on May 17, 1937, marked the beginning of regular production for the Model G. Even though it was the earliest *serial-numbered regular*-production G, G1004, a later-serial-numbered tractor actually was the first regular-production G built, being fully assembled on May 14, 1937 (the same day as G1000). Even though that is well ahead of the 1938 calendar year, Deere designated those earliest Gs as 1938 models, not 1937 models.

The Low-Radiator Problem

It wasn't very long after Deere had introduced the G that customers—particularly those in the southern plains—started experiencing problems with the powerhouse Model G overheating in the field. Deere ultimately combated the problem by enlarging the size of the radiator on the tractor. At the same time, modifications were also made to the radiator shutter assembly, fan shroud, and the fan. Since the new radiator was taller, the steering rod could not freely go over the radiator top tank. Thus, instead of incurring a lot of expense heightening the front pedestal of the tractor, Deere made additional (and less expensive, but just as effective) changes to the radiator top tank, molding a groove in the front edge that was just enough to allow the original steering shaft to pass through and attach to the original steering gear atop the original front pedestal. Because of the larger radiator, alterations to the tractor's hood and fuel tank were also necessary, among other things. These changes started as regular practice on tractor G4251.

Since regular production of the unstyled G started at serial number 1002 and the change to the larger radiator occurred at 4251, Deere originally produced less than 3250 "low-radiator" Gs. For Deere collectors, that has made

Deere didn't extend the styling as derived by Henry Dreyfuss & Associates to the G Series in the 1939 model year, as the model was still relatively new at that time. However, for the 1942 model year, Deere did extend the benefits of styling to the G Series, realizing that the competition already had streamlined tractors of similar horsepower in production by that time.

low-radiator Gs quite attractive in terms of collectibility. However, Deere was not content with the fact that they had solved the overheating problem for current-production tractors; the company also wanted to fix that problem on all previously produced Gs. Thus, Deere updated a large portion of the "low-radiator" Gs already in the field, giving them the new larger radiator and all of the other necessary related changes. Not many of those tractors avoided the update, so few original "low-radiator" Gs with the original radiator, hood, and related components exist. While it may not be too difficult for a collector today to locate an early G serial-numbered 4250 or lower, it is often a problem for them to find one that still has all of the original equipment. However, this means that "low-radiator" Gs that are still true low-radiator models are exceptionally rare today.

What's Missing Here?

For almost every other unstyled letter-series John Deere row-crop tractor series, there were eventually a variety of different configurations of that model designed to meet specific needs. Additionally, many of those original row-crop tractor series had standard-tread derivatives, as well. But, as is often the case, the G Series is an exception. Indeed, almost all of the unstyled G John Deeres were simply the Tricycle-type row-crops with dual, narrow-set front wheels. There were no regular-production unstyled Gs with either single front wheels (which would have been designated GNs) just as there were no regular-production unstyled Gs with wide adjustable front ends (which would have been called GWs). Similarly, there were also no standard-tread Gs (which would have been called GRs), for there really was no need for them. After all, John Deere already had the standard-tread Model D in production, and its horsepower was almost equal to that of the G anyway. Having two standard-tread tractors of equal horsepower wouldn't have made much sense, and the D was a strong enough seller on its own already.

1939 Comes and Goes, But the G Still Looks the Same

Most of the row-crop John Deeres underwent a styling revolution at the beginning of the 1939 model year, being adorned with new, eye-catching sheet metal. But it's no surprise that the G—often the exception—did not get a new look; it remained unstyled. The actual reasons for this decision are unknown, but some pretty good ideas have been proposed. For one, Deere had just introduced the G about one and one half years before 1939, so the company might have thought it too expensive to retool for a styled version of their powerhouse tractor. Furthermore, the G was not Deere's strongest seller, although it was arguably the most rugged of the row-crop Deeres.

A Move Toward Stylization

The G was supposed to be (and was) a very rugged, dependable tractor. It was made to work hard, and it did. For such a tractor, tractor companies long thought that what was most important to the tractor was how well it was built and how much work it could do, not what it looked like. But Deere & Company quickly realized how wrong that idea was, as sales of the archaic-looking Model G plummeted while the more stylish As and Bs still enjoyed strong sales. Likewise, most of the G's competition from other tractor brands was also quite stylish. For instance, International Harvester's Model M Farmall sported styled trim and a dashing red color, while Minneapolis-Moline's Model U with its classy teardrop hood side panels was very flashy in its bright Prairie Gold paint scheme with red trim. With those kinds of tractors taking a chunk out of Deere's sales in the three-plow tractor market, the company knew that the G had to be styled or perish.

As early as the spring of 1941, Deere started working on styling the G. The company decided to expand the styling as used on the row-crop Models A and B, thus allowing the G to fit in well with its brothers. Things progressed rather quickly, and by late 1941 Deere was ready to go with its new styled Model G, announcing the tractor with Decision 10000 of September 6, 1941. But Deere didn't stop at just styling the tractors; it did so very much more. And, indeed, by the time Deere decided it was finished with upgrading the model, it was obvious that what they really had was an all-new model on their hands. Thus, in the 1942 model year, Deere decided to release the Model GM.

The Model GM: The G Modernized

The designation for this all-new model came simply from amending what had been the Model G designation with the letter "M" for "Modernized." Deere built the GM to replace the G, and even though the GM was in many respects *similar* to the G, the GM was *very* different. It was truly a new model. In fact, the GM was so new that Deere used the following statement in its advertising literature: "A New and Finer JOHN DEERE 3-PLOW TRACTOR; Model 'GM'; *New* in its styled lines." Deere's Decision 10200 of February 26, 1942, states that "To better distinguish the improvement in the Model G Tractor, beginning with Serial Number G-13000, from the tractors made prior to that serial number, we will change the model designation from 'G' to 'GM.'"

Yes, the styling was a BIG deal. The new tractors looked almost identical to the early-styled John Deere Models A and B. The most notable difference in the GM's styling was that the air intake and exhaust stacks were still located across from each other on the hood, not in line with one another. Also, the GM retained the bulged front frame—just as on the unstyled Gs—which accommodated the large engine. Still, the GM was noticeably more appealing than its unstyled predecessors, just as the early-styled As and Bs had been in comparison to their forefathers.

As could be inferred from the wording of Decision 10200, sleek new lines weren't the only things that were new

about the new GM. Like the early-styled Model A, the GM also made use of a six-speed transmission, a feature that Decision 10000 also pointed out. Also, its engine benefited from the new "ramped" head design as was approved by Decision 10110 of January 15, 1942. That feature increased turbulence within the cylinders and thus improved the efficiency of the unit. This was a feature new to the Model A for the 1940 model year, one year after it was styled. That helps explain at least in part why the Model A wasn't replaced with an all-new model called the Model AM (for A Modernized); those changes were made in stages, not all at once.

There were a number of features that the GM was *supposed* to have as standard equipment that weren't always present. For instance, the six-speed transmission was supposed to be standard, but Deere would only allow the six-speed to be used in tractors equipped with rubber tires. That wasn't supposed to be a problem, either, as the GM was supposed to be fitted with rubber tires as standard practice, yet another new standard feature. Steel wheels were still available as special equipment, but when they were used the tractors would only be fitted with four-speed transmissions for safety's sake. However, rubber was the problem, as the government rationed rubber extensively during World War II. The military needed rubber in large quantities, as the product was needed for manufacturing the large tires of U.S. bomber aircraft such as the B-17 Flying Fortress and for a variety of other essential items. With the resultant restrictions on the use of rubber by both the public and companies, Deere and many other tractor companies were forced to produce numerous stylized tractors on less stylish steel wheels. For the Model GM, that

Deere wanted to bring special attention to its newly styled G Series tractors in the 1942 model year, and the best way to do that was to redesignate the model. Since Deere had modernized the G, the company decided to redesignate the model the Model GM for "G Modernized." The designation reverted back to simply "G" in 1947, as the company wanted the model's designation to be more consistent with the rest of the models in Deere's line. Shown is a 1950 late-styled G.

The unstyled Model G, like all of the other unstyled row-crop John Deere letter-series models, featured side-by-side air intake and exhaust stacks. These stacks should always be the same height, with the air intake stack being John Deere green and the exhaust stack being black.

also meant that a number of the tractors received four-speed transmissions, too.

Deere also made the GM available with electric starting and lighting equipment. However, many tractors received the conventional hand-crank flywheel, and a large number weren't fitted with lights, either. It is important to note that the hand-crank flywheel on the Model GM, though it had the same casting number as did the hand-crank flywheel on the unstyled G, was different from what it was before. Its outer lip was offset to the outside in order to accommodate a new bulge in the side of the transmission case that was necessary for the inclusion of fifth and sixth gears.

The Production of the GM: An Interesting History

While the last unstyled G, serial number 12192, had rolled out of the factory on December 22, 1941, the first GM did not see production until almost two full months later, on February 20, 1942. Obviously much retooling had to be done for production of the all-new GM. Deere & Company assigned serial number 13000 to the first GM, scrapping serial numbers 12193 through 12999 to make that possible.

Less than 750 tractors into production, Deere suspended GM production on September 21, 1942, the last unit being produced that day bearing serial number 13747. The cause was not the failure of the Model GM in any way. Instead, the GM was a casualty of World War II, as Deere felt it did not

When the Model G did receive its styling, it did not look exactly like an upscaled version of the Models B and A. The styled Models A and B received in-line exhaust stacks; however, that was not the case with the Model G.

Far right: Indeed, the Model G retained the old side-by-side design placement of its two stacks. The reason was due to the large size necessary in the G's components.

have sufficient materials to continue to produce the GM while still producing its other more popular row-crop tractors—the Models B and A.

While the roughly two-month break between unstyled G production and GM production seemed like a long time, it was short compared to the over two-year break in the middle of GM production. Deere reinstated the GM in late 1944, with the next tractor in the serial-number sequence—13758—rolling off the production line on October 16 as a 1945 model. By this time, Germany's industrial production had been bombed almost into submission and the D-Day invasion had been a success, meaning that the end of World War II was, for the first time, in sight. Thus, Deere felt confident that it could start to produce its GM again without any further complications resulting from the war.

In the year of production that followed the restart of GM production, Deere made over 2,000 GM tractors. With more tractors available, customers started buying them. And with the end of World War II in August 1945, even more tractors were sold. For the first postwar production year, 1946, well over 2,500 GMs were produced. In 1947, production was almost back to normal in comparison with prewar (pre-1939) levels.

The End of the GM

Following the close of World War II, the War Production Board, which had imposed the price regulations in the United States, dropped those regulations and things went back to normal for the tractor industry. Deere & Company was more than ready for the restrictions to be dropped, for more than one reason. One of those reasons included Deere's desire to make the designation of the styled G Series tractor, the GM, more consistent with that of the other tractors in Deere's line. As soon as Deere was presented the opportunity, it published Decision 12405 on September 19, 1946, announcing that the GM designation was going to be changed back to Model G. The Decision stated that this was to take place on or before February 1, 1947.

Thus, Deere terminated—once and for all—Model GM production in March 1947, the last GM bearing serial number 22112. Deere & Company scrapped serial numbers 22113 through 22999 so that production under the Model G would begin with serial number 23000.

The Model G (Re-)Introduced

Finally, the Model G was back! Deere finished the first of the styled Model Gs, serial number 23000, on March 7,

The late-styled Model G tractors did benefit from many of the same features Deere had upgraded the Models B and A with, including the battery-box seat with padded cushion and backrest. However, the G did not receive a pressed-steel frame, retaining the same frame style that had been in use since production's start.

1947, a little over a month after Decision 12405 anticipated. To begin with, the styled Gs were almost identical to the Model GMs that they replaced. Though they seldom do so, people could very well refer to these tractors as early-styled Gs, as they still very much resembled the early-styled Models A and B.

In June 1947, some 10 years and one month after Deere's introduction of the G Series, the Model G was again subjected to the tractor tests at the University of Nebraska. Deere submitted many of its tractor models to those tests right after they resumed production following the close of World War II, and in many cases the company enjoyed marked increases in horsepowers of tractor models that had previously been tested. However, in most of those cases, the engine size of the tractors had been boosted from their original specifications. For instance, the B's bore had been increased by 7/16 inch while its stroke had been lengthened by 1/4 inch. The Model A enjoyed a 1/4-inch longer stroke, as well. The G, however, possessed the same bore and stroke that it had during the 1937 tests. The principal engine-related improvement that the G had by 1947 was its ramped head engine design. It contributed to only slight increases in horsepower output as evidenced by the Nebraska Tests. The results of the 1947 tests revealed that the G could muster 27.08-rated drawbar horsepower and 34.2-rated and 36.03-maximum-load belt horsepowers.

Production of the early-styled G did not last very long. In all, Deere & Company produced around 2,500 of the units; the last early-styled G received serial number 25671. It is important to note that the production totals for the early-styled G included—for the first time—several new variations.

Two Variations Appear.
Finally: The Models GN and GW

Even though Deere had only produced the Model G in its original configuration from the beginning, the company had been producing single-front wheel and wide-adjustable front-axle versions of the Models A and B almost from the time they were introduced. Those versions of the A and B originally required the use of entire specialized front pedestals, which took both time and money to construct. However, beginning in the 1947 model year, Deere started using a new front pedestal assembly for the Models AN, AW, BN, and BW. This pedestal allowed front-end types to be interchanged by swapping only the bottom section of the new two-piece pedestals. Following the introduction of those tractors, Deere decided to go forward with enlarging the design of those "split" pedestals to fit the Model G. With that came the first two variations of the Model G—the Models GW and GN—which were introduced by Decisions 12401 and 12402, respectively, in early December 1946.

Deere didn't introduce specialized versions of the Model G quickly after production started as had been done with the Models A and B, but the Model G had different circumstances. Deere did not feel demand was high enough for a big 3-4 plow tractor to be specialized as had been the A and B, so the company didn't tool for any special versions for some time.

The paint scheme on the specialized versions of the Model G was nearly identical to that which Deere used on the basic Model G. Green paint with yellow wheels was just the beginning, though: the exhaust stacks and axles on these tractors should be painted black, for instance, and late-styled tractors could use either yellow or black seat cushions.

Below: By the 1947 model year, Deere did see enough limited demand for wide-front and narrow-front versions of the G to merit the introduction of the Models GW and GN. Those models were nearly identical to the basic Model G with the exception of the front ends.

The Late-Styled G Is Born

In July 1947, Deere released an even more refined version of the Model G. Production of these late-styled Model Gs began with serial number 26000; Deere had scrapped serial numbers 25672 to 25999 to make that possible.

These new tractors featured most of the improvements that adorned the updated late-styled Models A and B. For instance, a battery-box seat was used, and so discontinuing the use of the "MODEL G" designation stencil on the seat support channel. A new model designation stencil—the "G" in a circle—was used at this time and was located on the sides of each radiator grille screen in the recessed area. Also like the new As and Bs, the late-styled Gs no longer featured the "JOHN" and "DEERE" lettering on the left and right rear-axle housings, respectively, as read from the rear; instead, new square-shaped, flat-backed rear-axle housings were used.

Not surprisingly, though, the new Gs weren't larger versions of the late-styled Model A, as the Model G is almost always the exception to the rule. First, the flywheel on the G was not fully enclosed as it was on the A, nor did the G have its starter repositioned to the bottom of the crankcase. Thus, significant redesigns of the G crankcase were not necessary. What also set the G apart was that it was never advertised as being available with two different types of engines, one to burn gasoline and one to burn all-fuel; the G was only advertised as being available with all-fuel engines.

"Split" Pedestal Use Expanded

Conforming to practices just begun for the Model A, Deere expanded use of the two-piece "split" pedestal, which distinguished Models GN and GW, to the basic Model G in the 1950 model year. Thus, any 1950 or later Model G Series tractor could be fitted with the dual, narrow-set front-wheel assembly, the single-front wheel, or the wide-adjustable front axle.

One More Variation of the G Appears: Enter the Hi-Crop

Noting a need for a hi-crop–type tractor that had more power than the Model AH could produce, Deere opted to design the most specialized version of the Model G ever regularly produced. The new tractor—designated the Model GH—appeared in 1951 and had most of the same features as the slightly smaller Model AH hi-crop tractor. The Model GH received approval for production via Decision 15200

Aside from the basic row-crop, Deere produced only three variations of the G Series. The Model GH hi-crop tractor was by far the most noticeable, even at a distance.

Deere never bothered with producing simply high-clearance versions of the Model G; instead, the company went straight into producing a true hi-crop variation of the model. The Model GH served the role of the biggest and most powerful tractor in Deere's line that had been designed specifically for use in rice and cane fields.

The GH's drop boxes and long front spindles gave the model all of the boost it needed. Overall, the tractor cleared the ground by an impressive 33 inches—nearly 3 feet.

of March 2, 1950, which was to be made effective around August 1, 1950.

Deere's Model GH came standard with 12-38 six-ply rear tires, though 12-38 six-ply rice and cane tires were optional for the model. Deere installed 7.50x20 four-ply front tires on the GH as standard practice, as well, as was the case with the smaller Model AH tractor. Using the same six-speed transmission found in the regular Model G, the GH could travel at the following speeds with the standard 12-38 tires:

Speeds for the Model GH (12-38 rears)

Gear	Speed (mph)
First	2-1/4
Second	3-1/4
Third	4-1/4
Fourth	6
Fifth	8-1/4
Sixth	11-3/4
Reverse	3

Speeds for the GH when equipped with the optional 12-38 rice and cane rear tires increased by 1/4 mile per hour in all gears except sixth, where the speed increased a full 1/2 mile per hour.

Deere installed drop-box axle housings on the GH to give its rear axles an exceptional amount of ground clearance—an impressive 33 inches. Because the rear end of the tractor was so high off the ground, the model needed the three drawbar settings Deere gave it. The high setting put the drawbar 33 inches above the ground, whereas the center and low positions placed the drawbar height at 26 and 15 inches, respectively. Deere also designed special implements to work specifically with the Models GH and AH.

Since the GH used drop-box axle housings, rear tread adjustment couldn't be performed on this model as it was on the regular Model G. On the GH, one could only select from a set array of rear tread settings. These came in 6-inch steps from 60 to 90 inches. Front tread adjustment could only be done at set increments of 6 inches, also, but the tread range for it only extended from 60 to 84 inches.

The Close of Production

Production of the Model G ended permanently with serial number 64530 in February 1953. Deere introduced its Model 70 the next month as the replacement for the Model G.

The Model G was the largest of the row-crop letter-series John Deeres, and its production history is unique among those tractors. The G had retained the same engine size throughout its entire production run, as it was one of the few tractors of its era that did not benefit from increased bores or lengthened strokes. In reality, the G never

needed them, as it was always a tough workhorse, standing as one of the most rugged tractors ever produced by any company.

Of the row-crop letter-series John Deeres, the G was available with the fewest variations if you exclude the Model GM. In all, including the basic model, which comprised most of the series' production, the G was only available in four different application styles: G (including GM), GN, GW, and

GH. There were never standard-tread or industrial variations of the G available in regular production, even though standard-tread versions were experimented with and predicted for production by Deere at one time.

Nonetheless, collecting Model Gs can be very rewarding and often challenging. To compile a complete collection of the most notable different types of the G would take a considerable amount of time and money. Such a collection would consist of the low-radiator unstyled G; a large-radiator unstyled G; a GM; one each of the early-styled Models G, GN, and GW; one each of the late-styled Models G, GN, and GW; and one Model GH. In all, that's only 10 tractors, which doesn't sound like too many. However, when one considers how hard it is to find about half of those tractors, it makes one appreciate the Model G for the challenges collecting it offers collectors.

Despite the short list of variations of the Model G, the series still is popular with many collectors. The G is also very popular with tractor pullers as well; as the model usually hangs tough in the 6,500-pound class.

The Model L Series

Understanding the Model L Series John Deere tractors fully requires one to take a mental trip back in time. We must consider history on at least two different levels, that of producers and that of consumers. Specifically, we will often think from the perspective of tractor manufacturers, particularly Deere & Company, and farmers.

Let's start our journey from the beginning of regular tractor production by Deere & Company. While the Great War was raging in Europe, Deere purchased the Waterloo Gasoline Engine Company and took over production of the Waterloo Boy tractors in March 1918. That was a move that put Deere in the tractor business for good.

For Deere, the timing of the Waterloo purchase couldn't have been better. The purchase meant that Deere did not have to spend valuable time and money experimenting with tractor designs, and it also meant that Deere didn't have to spend large sums of money on introductory sales literature. The Waterloo Boy tractors already had proven themselves as reliable machines, and their name was already well recognized in the agricultural realm.

Those considerations are important for any tractor company at any time, but they were particularly vital for Deere in the late 1910s. On April 6, 1918, approximately three years and eight months after World War I actually started, the U.S. Congress declared war on Germany, marking the United States' official entry into the war. The U.S. government initiated the War Industries Board to regulate the U.S. wartime economy. This organization, coupled with the passing of the Lever Food and Fuel Control Act, in part regulated farm output.

During World War I, the United States was faced with the not-so-easy job of feeding not only U.S. citizens but those of Europe, as well, as agricultural activity in that area had dwindled significantly due to the war. The U.S. government thus encouraged farmers to purchase and put into cultivation as much land as possible so that more food would be produced. In America's free-market economy, an overproduction of food would have normally caused prices of those goods to plummet, but this was avoided as the U.S government imposed price restraints and subsidized farming.

There were certainly other, though less significant ways, that U.S. citizens could help feed Europe. In fact, the government strongly encouraged housewives to cook meals that would conserve food, keeping alive the prevalent theme "Food [Would] Win The War" as many promotional posters of the era proclaimed. However, the most important way to increase food production to feed the masses was through cultivation of more land.

At the time, many farms in the United States still made active use of animal power, as the tractor and other advancements in agricultural technology were still rather new. However, the U.S. government recognized the advantages of mechanized agriculture, so it urged farmers to buy tractors and take advantage of the labor-saving, more efficient new farm equipment of the time. As a result, demand for those products increased, and farm equipment companies reacted.

In 1919 there was a flurry of activity, particularly in the area of tractor production. There were those companies that were already selling tractors, those companies that had toyed with the idea of selling tractors before with little success, and those companies that had never before made a tractor or anything like one but wanted to participate in the emerging, booming business. In all, it has been estimated that around 200 companies were producing tractors for the 1919 model year, many of which were not preexisting models or even brands, for that matter.

The brand-new companies had the severe disadvantage of not having an established, recognized name or a product with proven reliability. They shouldered the additional burden of having to start their tractor designs from scratch, with no guarantee that they would work well. And, furthermore, since their products were not known, they also had to spend large sums of money on introductory advertising in order to be successful.

While things weren't necessarily easy for Deere during this period, at least the company had a well-proven and well-known tractor—the Waterloo Boy—to sell. What's more, the company also benefited from the experimental models that the Waterloo Gasoline Engine Company was developing at the time of the Deere purchase. Deere had a leg up on

Opposite: The Model L Series tractors and their predecessors featured an all-new design, differing drastically from the established trends in Deere tractors at the time. They fit the small-tractor market well, however, and will go down in history as one of the most notable John Deere tractors.

the competition, many of which would soon appear to have been ridden hard and put away wet.

The problems for many of Deere's competitors began right after the close of World War I on November 11, 1919. The U.S. government dropped the price restraints on U.S. farm commodities, but farmers kept right on producing at the wartime levels. With the war over, that much food was no longer needed, so a surplus of farm goods quickly materialized. As a result, by 1921, farm prices had plummeted. Agriculture in the United States was now in a state of economic depression after years of booming business during the World War I.

With farm prices at an unbelievable low, the demand for farm products dropped sharply. Many of the new companies that had invested so much money getting started couldn't sell enough of their not-so-well-known products, and as a result many of them went bankrupt or simply terminated production. Deere, as well as the majority of the other established farm tractor companies, struggled through these tougher-than-usual times and continued production. Furthermore, in many cases, experimentation with new designs continued.

Yet another factor that helped Deere and most of the other proven tractor brands was the formation of the University of Nebraska Tractor Tests late in 1919, with the first tests concluding in 1920. Since there were so many new and unproven tractor brands that had surfaced during World War I, it was often the case that the newer tractor companies simply threw together their models with little or no testing for reliability. While sales of these tractors did not significantly hurt the sales of companies such as Deere, they

still took away part of what would have been additional income. Thus, the Nebraska Tractor Tests brought credibility to the tractor market, and this likely led to the demise of many of the fly-by-night companies. For Deere, however, the tests stood as yet another testimonial of the reliability of their products.

Up to this point, we have seen how Deere placed itself firmly in the tractor market with its Model D. We have also seen how the company expanded its grasp to the row-crop tractor market through the Models C, GP, GPWT, and eventually the highly successful Models A and B. After the B's introduction, however, Deere still wasn't content with the extent of its row-crop line. The company wanted both a tractor bigger than the A and a tractor smaller than the B. The engineers at Waterloo quickly got to work, designing the eventual Model G to fill the big end of the spectrum. That project would be realized in 1937 with the G's introduction. For Waterloo, though, the attempts to make a smaller general-purpose row-crop modeled after the Model B would not be fully realized until 1939. That tractor, the H, would actually serve to fill the gap that would be left by the B's increase in power, as the H ultimately produced within about one horsepower of what the B originally had produced on steel in 1935.

To really satisfy Deere's desire for a tractor smaller than the B—both in size and horsepower—Deere turned to the John Deere Wagon Works in the hometown of the company, Moline, Illinois. This move made sense, as Deere was looking for a nonconventional tractor, something unlike any tractors previously produced bearing the John Deere name. The only requirements set forth were that the tractor have a two-cylinder engine and a small price tag.

The Model Y is perhaps the most interesting of the John Deere letter-series tractors. These tractors were assembled from various different parts by hand, but no original units are known to be in existence to this day. *Deere & Company Archives*

The Model Y

In order to reduce the costs of experimentation, the Wagon Works tried to make use of preexisting products in assembling the first of these new one-row tractors. They would become known as the Model Ys, which were built during the 1936 production year. Furthermore, these tractors were not produced in the usual fashion; instead, they were *assembled* by hand. In all, 24 Ys were built.

To begin with, the Ys made use of a Novo engine. However, Deere started using a Hercules-built engine—the Model NXA—partway through the Y production. Both were two-cylinder engines, but they were of a different design from what Deere was accustomed to—they were not horizontally oriented. Instead, the engines were mounted upright, with the crankshaft pointing straight ahead of the operator, not lying down crosswise in front. This was done to cut down on the width of the tractor, as one of its principal uses would be cultivating, which is easier to do if the operator can see forward more readily.

Due to the positioning of the engine on the Y, these tractors were not started by grabbing hold of the flywheel and turning it over by hand. Instead, the Y was started much like cars of the period, by using a hand crank located at the front of the tractor. This same basic style of manual starting would be used on the successors of the Y until production's end, though electric starting would eventually become available.

For the transfer of power between the engine and the differential, the Y made use of a Ford Model A car transmission. Even though it gave the tractor a shifting pattern not normally found on Deere tractors of the era, this would eventually become a selling point for the tractor. After all, its shift pattern was just like that of a car!

The engine and transmission of the Y were both mounted on the tractor's steel tube frame. This entire chassis of the tractor was basically in one piece, including the front frame and rear-end/rear axle housings. This basic design would be used on this model's successors until their demise.

The Model 62

Deere started production of the replacement for the Y—the Model 62—in early 1937. The first Model 62 bore serial number 621000, and production ended later in 1937 with number 621078. Thus, it is estimated that approximately 79 Model 62 tractors were produced.

The Model L Series started out as an experimental tractor with a letter designation: the Model Y. Replacing it was the Model 62, but that numbered designation didn't stick around for long in Deere's predominantly lettered tractor model line.

It didn't take long for the Model 62 to evolve into the Model L. Shown here is the last Model 62, serial number 621078, and the first Model L, serial number 621079. The Model L is distinguishable from the 62 in lacking the JD logo cast into the front end.

Perhaps the most noticeable difference between the Model L and the rest of Deere's letter-series tractors at the time was its tubular-type frame. Besides the L, the rest of the tractors either featured a channel-iron-type frame (or front-end support) that bolted into the main case casting (as used on the Model A, for instance) or no frame at all, such as the Model D.

The Model 62 was far more stylish-looking than its predecessor. The most notable new feature of this model was the front shield located beneath the radiator. This boldly showed the John Deere "JD" logo cast into it, though for some unknown reason this feature was not painted yellow to give it additional contrast with the tractor. The same logo was also cast into the rear end/rear axle housing on the back of the tractor.

Also different on the Model 62 were its fenders. The Y had had full fenders that extended over the tops of the rear tires, but those fenders were simply flat on the inside and abruptly bent at a 90-degree angle to cover the tops of the tires. On the 62, the tire tops were still covered by the full fenders, but they did not have the abrupt bend in them; instead, there was a gentler curve in the fenders at that point.

There were further differences between the Models 62 and the Y. For instance, the Y featured a steel seat with a full backrest, armrests, and a cushion. The 62 simply made use of the same style of pan-type steel seat as used on Deere production tractors of its time. Furthermore, the 62 used a three-spoke steering wheel (as opposed to the Y's four-spoke wheel) and entirely different rear wheels.

Another important new feature of the Model 62 was the location of its transmission. Instead of being attached to the rear of the engine, like the Model Y, it was placed directly in front of the rear-axle housing and differential.

The Model L

Late in 1937, Deere decided to make changes to what had been the Model 62 and also change its designation to be more consistent with the lettered models in Deere's line. As a result, the Model L was born.

The Model L used the same serial-number run that the Model 62 had started. The first L picked up exactly where the 62 had left off, beginning with serial number 621079. What's more, the unstyled L continued to use the same engine—the Hercules NXA—as the 62 had utilized.

The first thing one often notices about the original unstyled Model Ls is that they do not feature the JD logo cast into the front-end shield and the rear-axle housing. While that arguably made the unstyled L less stylish than the 62, the fenders of the L made up the difference. On the L, these did not extend all the way over the tops of the rear tires, but they were far more curved, making them resemble clamshell-type fenders.

Deere & Company made available special industrial versions of the unstyled Model L, though these tractors did not officially receive the Model LI designation (that would affect later tractors, though). In general, the industrial unstyled Ls were almost identical to the agricultural versions of the model; the most common difference was the presence of paint other than John Deere green—typically industrial yellow.

The Styled L

For the 1939 model year, the little Model L followed suit with most of Deere's row-crop tractors, being

released in new, more stylish sheet metal. Even though the L had only been in production for one year by that time, Deere decided to go forward with the styling of this model. The new tractors used a serial-number run beginning at 625000.

Since the Model L's design was so unique and so compact, it did not receive exactly the same styling lines as had

Deere & Company only produced the Model L in an unstyled form for one year. Then, in 1939, the styled versions of that model appeared.

Aside from the obvious differences in sheet metal, perhaps the quickest way to distinguish between the unstyled and styled Model Ls is to look at the wheels. The styled Model L's wheels had no cutouts, unlike those used on the unstyled L and 62.

the Models A, B, and H in 1939. The new L design didn't really have a true hood, but rather an engine cover. That cover, nonetheless, did bear some resemblance to the hoods used on the aforementioned tractors. However, the L's engine cover curved down around behind the engine, as well. And, since the L did not have a front pedestal, it did not have the same style of casting running down the front of the radiator grille screen as did the A, B, and H.

Powering the styled Model L was another Hercules engine, this time the Model NXB. Its upright two-cylinder engine featured a 3-1/4x4-inch bore and stroke, which gave the engine a total displacement of approximately 66 cubic inches. Deere rated the engine at 1,550 rpm.

In mid-November 1938, the John Deere Model L underwent testing at the University of Nebraska. The tested tractor was serial number 625030 with engine number 422811. In test 313, this tractor produced a rated 9.28 belt horsepower and a maximum load belt horsepower of 10.42. On the drawbar, it also produced a rated 7.06 horsepower and a maximum load horsepower of 9.06.

Changes to the Styled Model L

The styled Model L underwent a variety of changes, some of which were very important.

Transmission

After scrapping 500 serial-number plates at the end of the 1939 model year, Deere introduced the 1940 Model Ls, starting at serial number 629000. The most significant improvement on these tractors was the new transmission of John Deere's own design. This transmission replaced the original Spicer transmission, though the shifting pattern remained the same on the new unit. However, due to a slightly different design, the gearshift lever came out of the right side of the transmission (instead of the top as on the Spicer), thus requiring a bend in the lever to make it vertical.

Engine

At the end of the 1940 model year, Deere again scrapped a large run of serial-number plates, this time consisting of numbers 634841 to 639999. This was done so that the 1941 model tractors would start production at the nice, rounded-off number of 640000. The reason? Principally, it was because the Model L was to feature a new John Deere–produced engine to take the place of the Hercules. That first tractor was produced on July 17, 1941.

The new engine had some new features, as well. For one, the block and crankcase of the engine were cast in the same piece with the flywheel housing, whereas those pieces had been cast separately on the Hercules engines. Additionally, the breather tube on the new John Deere engine stuck out from underneath the tractor's sheet metal because it was set at an angle. On the Hercules, the breather tube was set vertically, thus it did not protrude.

Styled Model L Variations

By far the most popular of the styled Model Ls was the agricultural version. However, Deere & Company produced other special variations of that model over the years.

Styled Model LIs, which are painted yellow, are usually Model LIs, unless, of course, someone simply decided to paint an agricultural model yellow.

Even though Deere did produce industrial-type Ls prior to the 1941 model year, those tractors are not officially Model LIs. Thus, no unstyled L, whether an industrial or not, should technically be called an LI.

The Model L Hi-Clearance

In the midst of the 1939 model year, a new version of the Model L appeared. This tractor probably could have been called the Model LH in order to be consistent with the model designation meanings Deere was using on the high-clearance Models A, B, and H at the time; however, Deere never used that designation for these tractors. The Hi-Clearance L earned its name by using longer front spindles, 15-inch front tires (either 4.00x15 or 5.00x15), and 7.50x22-inch rear tires instead of the 6.00x22-inch tires that came standard on the normal L.

The Model LI

The Model L had been sold as industrial tractors clear back from the model's introduction, with unstyled versions even sporting the industrial yellow paint schemes. However, these tractors were sometimes simply agricultural models painted industrial yellow (or other special colors), and they were included in the midst of the serial-number run as used by the agricultural Ls. These were not specifically referred to as the Model LIs for quite some time. Clearly orchestrating the existence of these tractors is the Serial Number Registers for the Model L at Deere & Company Archives, a document that lists—in some cases—when special paint colors were applied to the styled Model L. Here is some of the information gleaned from that document:

Model Ls Painted Special Colors

625073	= yellow
625075	= highway yellow
625079	= highway yellow
625388	= yellow
625389	= yellow
627101	= yellow
627123 to 627126	= yellow
627128 to 627134	= yellow
627136 to 627147	= yellow
627868 to 627892	= yellow
629062 to 629064	= yellow
629067	= yellow
633035 to 633039	= burnt orange
633341	= special yellow
633344	= special yellow
633348	= special yellow
633358 to 633360	= special yellow
633361	= special orange
633362	= Tenn. orange
633363	= Tenn. orange
633364	= special color
633370 to 633376	= Tenn. orange

Model LI tractors came in very handy for highway departments when mowing ditches. A side-mounted sickle mower thus appeared on a number of these tractors. Here we can see that the mower's sickle bar could be fastened in an upright position to allow for down-the-road travel.

While the front hubs on the agricultural versions of the styled Model L were painted green, like the main body of the tractor, the hubs on the styled LIs were painted black, which was the trim color for that model.

Even though the Model L's engine was easy to hand start, especially compared with models such as the D, the electric starter served as a popular option for this model.

Like most John Deere letter-series industrial tractors, the LI could be ordered with special colors, not just yellow with black trim. Orange was perhaps the second most common color found on these units.

Beginning with the 1941 model year, the Model LI became an official tractor in Deere's growing line. The model was assigned a new serial-number run, starting with number 50001. Along with the different designation and serial-number run came different features, as well. They featured higher-geared transmissions, a strengthened front axle with shorter spindles that gave the tractor a shorter yet wider stance, special rear-wheel spacers that were used to increase rear tread width, and a larger-sized gasoline tank that increased operating time. The LI continued in production through the 1946 model year, though it is interesting to note that it was the only John Deere industrial tractor made during those years.

The Model LI is interesting in that it appeared in a variety of paint schemes. Fortunately, the Serial Number Registers for the LI (which are kept at Deere & Company Archives) do indicate in many instances when special paint colors were used. Here is some of that information as gleaned from that document:

Model LIs with Special Paint Colors
50360 = yellow
50361 = yellow
50362 = yellow
50363 = yellow
50364 = yellow
50365 = yellow
50366 = yellow
50367 = yellow
50418 = Tenn. (possibly Tennessee Orange)
50419 = Tenn. (possibly Tennessee Orange)
50420 = Tenn. (possibly Tennessee Orange)
50421 = Tenn. (possibly Tennessee Orange)
50422 = Tenn. (possibly Tennessee Orange)
52018 = green
52019 = green

The Model Ls with Special Low-Clearance Front Axles

The Deere & Company Serial Number Registers for the Model L reveal that some of those tractors were fitted with a special low-clearance–type front axle, though no particulars are given. The following tractors are noted as having a low axle or being of the low-clearance type:

Model Ls with Low-Clearance Features
631538
632423 to 632429
632496
632608
632610 to 632612
632615
633857

Other Special Model Ls

Evidence in the Serial Number Registers of Deere & Company Archives also suggests that there was at least one Model L, number 633714, that had a special 48-inch tread and one, number 634072, that was fitted with 51-inch axles.

An All-New Model: The LA

Also new for 1941 was an all-new model of the L Series. This tractor—the Model LA—was quite different from the regular L, and many often think that it replaced the L. Not so. Indeed, these two tractors were produced simultaneously until production's end in 1946. The LA made use of its own serial-number run, which began at number 1001. The first two or three LAs were built in August 1940, but production did not resume until January 1941.

Perhaps the quickest way to distinguish a Model LA from an L is to look at the rear wheels. The L had pressed-steel rear wheels with attached rims. The LA, on the other hand, had cast centers with demountable rims and used attaching lugs similar to those found on tractors such as the Models A, B, and G. Typically, the rims of the LA were painted silver, not dark gray or yellow as had been normally done on the L. It is also important to note that the LA came standard with 24-inch rear wheels instead of 22-inch wheels like those of the L.

With the Model LA, Deere proved that you can pack big things in small packages. For its size, the LA packed plenty of power, giving it about a 4-horsepower edge over its brother, the styled L.

The rear wheels on the Model L underwent changes right along with the series. The original wheel type used on the Model 62 and unstyled L is seen in this photo.

When the company released the styled Model L in 1939, Deere dropped the original cast wheels with cutouts from the model series in favor of the wheel type seen below.

Another important feature of the Model LA was that its frame was made of round bar stock instead of steel tubing. With the additional mass of the round bar stock came an increased weight for the tractor. That meant that wheel weights didn't have to be used as often, as traction had been increased simply by the new frame mass. There have been LAs found with the steel tubing frames, as well, but this was not usually the case, and most of the exceptions are early tractors.

The Model LA also stood taller than the standard L. The LA took advantage of the same front-end features that came on the Hi-Clearance versions of the L, thus increasing front-end clearance.

While all these features are ways to distinguish a Model LA from an L, they are not the most important difference between the two models. What really made the LA stand out was that it was considerably more powerful than the L. This was achieved in part by Deere's increasing the bore of the tractor's engine from 3-1/4 inches to 3-1/2 inches. That boosted engine displacement from about 66 to around 77 cubic inches. Additionally, Deere boosted the engines on the LA by 300 rpm, resulting in a rated engine speed of 1,850 rpm.

Tweaking of the engine certainly helped. At the University of Nebraska, LA number 1229 cranked out a rated

The later Model LA, which starting in 1941 Deere produced simultaneously along with the styled L, used different rear wheels from the other L Series tractors. The Model LA's wheels had visible lugs to attach the wheel centers to the detachable rims.

The wheels on the Model LI were nothing like those used on the LA. However, one must keep in mind that industrial versions of the LA were produced, though not called LAIs. Those tractors likely had wheel styles like those used on the regular LA.

belt horsepower of 12.97 (as opposed to 9.28 for the L) and a maximum load belt horsepower of 14.34 horsepower (as opposed to 10.42 for the L). Drawbar horsepower results showed similar increases over the L, with the LA producing an impressive 10.62 rated load horsepower and as much as 13.10 drawbar horsepower in the maximum load tests. Those ratings were about 3 to 4 more horsepower than what the L had previously produced.

The Special Model LAs

While there are likely a number of Model LAs that have special features, little is known about them. Here is some information on a few of those special kinds of tractors.

The Industrial-Type LAs

No known evidence indicates that there were ever Model LAI tractors produced, but there were a few LAs

that did appear with industrial-type features. Furthermore, some LAs were likely painted industrial yellow, though no known records indicate which tractors received that paint scheme.

The Model LAs with Special Rear Axles

The Serial Number Registers for the Model L at Deere & Company Archives indicate that three Model LAs were fitted with special 51-inch rear axles, probably the same as those on certain Model Ls as discussed previously. Only the serial numbers of these tractors are known: 2053, 2054, and 2126.

The End of L Production

The end of the Model L Series production came at the last part of the 1946 model year. The next year, Deere would introduce the Model M Series to help fill the gap left by the discontinuation of the L Series.

The Model H Series

By 1937, Deere's smallest tractors were the Model B and the newly introduced Model L. The Model B was of the conventional row-crop general-purpose design, while the Model L's design was unique to John Deere tractors, resembling a garden tractor. In 1937, the B still had the same 4-1/4x5-1/4-inch bore and stroke that it had started production with, and that engine was rated at 14.3 belt horsepower. The smaller L used a Hercules engine with a 3x4-inch bore and stroke. But the sizes of both of those engines, as we will see, would soon change.

Something else important happened in 1937, as well. In that year, Deere approached Henry Dreyfuss & Associates about styling Deere's tractors. At around the same time, Deere also began toying with the idea of increasing the engine sizes of both the Models L and the B; even the Model A was considered for an engine size increase.

Indeed, Deere & Company did go forward with increasing the horsepower of many of its tractor models. The Model A, which started production in 1934 being able to deliver only 24.71 brake horsepower under maximum load, could bring 28.93 brake horsepower to bear under similar conditions with the arrival of the styled Model A in the fall of 1938. Deere then called on the Model B to step up and more adequately fill the resulting horsepower gap between it and the A. Thus, in the fall of 1938 the B's power was boosted to 18.53 brake horsepower under maximum load, a figure that was up slightly from the 16.01 that the B was originally capable of delivering.

When one considers the horsepower of the Models A, B, and G as they existed in the fall of 1938, it becomes apparent that there were nearly even horsepower differences between the models. The A was roughly 10.5

Opposite: Size-wise, the Model H ranked right at the bottom of the Deere conventional row-crop lineup. The smaller Model L used a different chassis design, and the L took the honors of being the smallest-horsepowered tractor in Deere's line; the H ranked second in that category.

Deere started experimentation on its Model OX with the unit in unstyled form. The most important difference in this model when compared with Deere's other tractors at the time is its rearward-slanting front pedestal. However, the model soon took on the stylized sheet metal that appeared on the Models A and B at the beginning of the 1939 model year.
Deere & Company Archives

Before the OX resulted in a production tractor, it too had been affected by the "Dreyfuss touch." Note that the styled Model OX no longer had the star-shaped rear-wheel centers and the backward-swept front pedestal and steering rod support column that its unstyled predecessor had, making this model look much more like the other row-crops in Deere's line at the time. *Deere & Company Archives*

horsepower more powerful than the B, and the G outpowered the A by about 7 horsepower. Deere noticed that the gap between the A and B was bigger, so it is not surprising that the B was given even more power in 1940 via an increased compression ratio and a larger delivering-capacity fuel system. With that change, the B was only about 9 horsepower less than the A.

Deere anticipated the boosting of horsepower in the Models A and B, and since they knew how successful the Model B previously had been in the general-purpose one-plow market, the company felt it was necessary to retain a general-purpose row-crop tractor designed specifically for that category. The L simply wouldn't do, as its design was more specific and, thus, did not fulfill the "general purpose" aspect that Deere desired in that category. So, by late 1937, Deere began experimenting with a new general-purpose tractor to fill the gap that would be made when the horsepower of the Model B was increased.

The new experimental units that Deere designed in its move to fill that gap became known as the Model OXs. While these tractors resembled the unstyled Models A, B,

and G, there were many notable differences. Perhaps the most unusual characteristics of the OX were its rearward-slanting front pedestal and rear steering shaft support. Another notable oddity of the OX was that its rear-wheel centers—with mounted rims and rubber tires—were cast iron and resembled a five-pointed star with curved edges. Other unusual features included the OX's bowed-metal seat spring (instead of the usual seat support with a coiled spring at its base) and the positioning of both the air intake and exhaust stacks on the left-hand side of the steering shaft.

In the summer of 1938, when Deere's first styled 1939 models rolled off the line, the company decided to go ahead and extend the styling to the Model OX, which would very soon lead to the regular-production Model H.

The H Starts, Then Sputters

Production of the John Deere Model H first started with serial number 1000 on October 29, 1938. Production of the H was approved by Decision 7900 on September 30, 1938, which also outlined the features of the model. According to that Decision, the H—which was intended for use on

small farms or for small, odd jobs on larger farms—was to have a three-speed transmission providing governed forward speeds of 2.55, 3.52, and 5.83 miles per hour.

While the Model H would soon become known for giving reliable service, the model did have one early setback. The first 104 Hs, serial-numbered 1000 to 1103, were fitted with a cast alloy iron crankshaft. Unlike most of the crankshafts in the other tractors in Deere's line (which had forged steel crankshafts), the cast alloy crankshaft didn't seem to satisfy Deere's expectations. Deere's Decision 8081 of November 28, 1938, stated that those crankshafts sometimes experienced what Deere called a "fatigue fracture" and called for changes to correct the problem. Thus, Deere had those 104 tractors returned, and most of them were eventually scrapped.

The Model H Production Restarted

To remedy the Model H's problem of the weak cast alloy iron crankshafts, Deere decided to replace them with the conventional forged steel–type crankshaft that Deere had been using successfully for years in most of its other tractors.

With the new crankshaft added, production resumed on January 18, 1939, with serial number 1104. This tractor is considered the first regular-production Model H.

The Model H was fitted with a horizontal, two-cylinder engine that, on the surface, closely resembled those used in the other general-purpose letter-series Deere tractors. Its engine, with its 3-9/16x5-inch bore and stroke providing right around 100 cubic inches of displacement, was rated at 1,400 rpm. At the University of Nebraska Tractor Tests in Test 312, the H developed 13.01 belt horsepower and 9.77 drawbar horsepower under rated load. The operating maximum load tests showed the H with a top-end output of 14.22 belt horsepower and 11.67 drawbar horsepower. It is interesting to note that the Model H that was tested was the very first H, serial number 1000—one of the tractors with the unsuccessful cast alloy iron crankshaft.

When considering the horsepower of the Model H at the start of its production, it becomes obvious that the H did a wonderful job of filling the gap that the B had left in the general-purpose one-plow tractor category in Deere's line. In truth, the H started production being able to deliver only 2

The Model H John Deere tractor could be used for all sorts of small jobs on large farms, but it was powerful enough to serve as the principal workhorse on a number of smaller farms, as well. The list of options for the model gave customers a wide selection to customize their H to best fit their needs.

horsepower less than the B had originally been able to put out in 1934. And, in 1939, the H was only about 4 horse-power less powerful than the B was, though that difference would increase to about 5 horsepower the next year when the B was again upgraded.

The transmission of the Model H was a three-speed unit providing forward speeds of around 2-1/2, 3-1/2, and 5-3/4 miles per hour and one reverse speed of 1-3/4 miles per hour. Furthermore, the H could attain a relatively fast trans-port speed of 7.5 miles per hour in third gear by overriding the governor with the accelerator foot pedal, an act that sped the engine up to as much as 1,800 rpm. Those speeds were provided when the tractor was fitted with 7-1/2x32-inch rear tires that were made standard shortly after production began. The standard front tires were 4.00x15 inches. Since steel wheels were not optional on the H, it was the only general-purpose row-crop in Deere's line to lack that option.

Despite how different the unstyled Model OX had looked in comparison to the unstyled Model B, the Model H fit in well with its larger row-crop brothers. The H used the same basic styling lines, including the striking front grille, and had the same-style rear-wheel centers and seat support as the larger Deere tractors. There were, however, a few outer characteristics of the H that made it dis-tinguishable from its big brothers.

The most striking difference between the Model H and the rest of the general-purpose Deeres was that it only had one stack protrud-ing from the top of the hood. That exhaust stack came out of the center of the hood, just as it did on the other tractors. However, there was no air intake stack present. To accommodate the in-take of air for carburetion, Deere provided an opening on the left side of the hood toward the front that was protected by a wire screen. With stencils placed properly, this opening should be just ahead of the "J" in the "JOHN DEERE" hood stencil.

Though introduced in 1939, the Model H did not bear the "JOHN" and "DEERE" letter-ing as cast into the left and right rear-axle hous-ings as found on the Models B, A, and G. This was likely done because of the small size of the H's housings.

For the Model Hs produced up to serial number 47795 at the end of the 1943 model year, there is one more way to spot these trac-tors. Those earlier Model Hs featured cast front-wheel centers that had five oval cutouts to-ward the outside edges, a design unique to those tractors. However, beginning with serial number 47796 at the beginning of the 1945 model year (please see explanation of the jump in model years toward the end of this chapter), the H was

A one-plow tractor, the Model H delivered as much as 14.84 brake horsepower and 12.48 drawbar horsepower at the Nebraska Tractor Tests. While plowing could be done with this model, farmers typically chose to do cultivation activities or other comparably light work with this tractor; its agility in the field was amazing.

Deere's Model H came on the scene wearing the sharpest clothes Deere could find, adorning the model in very striking apparel. The H never saw production in an unstyled form, a first for a John Deere tractor.

The Model H never featured an air intake stack; the only stack that protruded from its hood was the exhaust stack. The engine received the air it needed via the opening in the side of the hood as seen in this photo.

The basic Model H featured two distinct front wheels during its production. Early models used the cast front wheel with five oval cutouts as seen on the tractor at the left, while later models such as the tractor seen here on the right used pressed-steel front wheels without cutouts.

fitted with pressed-steel front wheels much like those available on the other Deere general-purpose tractors.

Mentioning only the unique external characteristics of the Model H would merely be scraping the surface of the H's individuality. Some of the most interesting differences between this model and its larger brothers in the Deere line were internal, meaning that little or no evidence of their presence can be noted by simply viewing the surface of these units.

The Model H Engine Operation

While still of the same horizontal two-cylinder design that Deere had become noted for, the engine of the Model

H did not deliver its power in the same manner as its relatives in the Deere lineup did. To understand the reason why this was so, one must first understand at least part of the process of engine operation.

On the previous two-cylinder John Deeres, power was delivered directly from the crankshaft to the clutch. This meant that each time the crankshaft made a full revolution, the clutch/belt pulley made a full revolution. This system was effective in delivering the desired amount of horsepower in a two-cylinder engine for a variety of reasons. For one, the engines had big bores and long strokes—a combination that provided enough torque on the crankshaft to produce enough horsepower. Second, these engines made enough horsepower that they did not have to be operated at high speeds in order to turn the crankshaft and the belt pulley at speeds most conducive to powering belt-driven equipment off the clutch pulley. Had the clutch pulley turned too fast (the desired belt speed was less than 3,200 feet per minute in most cases), would have been a tendency for the belt to slip and fall off.

The Model H, however, was a small tractor, so it had a small engine. Its small 3-9/16x5-inch bore would have to be operated at a quite fast rpm in order to produce the desired horsepower. Had the power been delivered from the

crankshaft in the conventional manner, the clutch pulley would have turned too fast to deliver the desired and necessary belt speed. Deere deemed it necessary to provide one step of gear reduction between the crankshaft and the clutch pulley. That was done by transferring power through the camshaft, a move that caused a 2:1 gear reduction. Furthermore, that doubled the torque delivered to the clutch pulley, which helped considering that the clutch pulley had to be increased in diameter in order to speed up the belt speed, as the 2:1 reduction had actually made the belt speed slower than it should have been. In the end, by delivering the power via the camshaft instead of the crankshaft, Deere made the H do what it was intended to do.

One notable effect of running the clutch pulley off the camshaft—which turned in the opposite direction as the crankshaft—was that the clutch pulley turned counterclockwise, instead of clockwise as on most other tractors. This made it necessary to twist endless belts one-half turn in order to properly power remote belt-driven equipment.

To reduce costs, Deere eliminated the final drive bull gears and shafts in the Model H. This meant that the brakes, while operated off the differential bull gear shafts in most Deeres to that point, had to be connected directly onto the rear-axle shafts.

Deere's Model HN appeared on the market in 1940, just one year after Deere had introduced the H. The narrow-front HN differed from the basic H only by having a single-front wheel and front-end yoke.

Below left: The Model HN's single-front wheel made cultivation of narrowly spaced row crops—an activity that the H Series performed often—much easier than it had been with the conventional, dual-wheeled, narrow-set front end of the original H.

The Model H featured tremendous operator visibility, made possible in part by the single stack protruding from the tractor's hood.

Variations of the Model H

Deere produced a few different versions of the Model H during its production run. All H versions were of the row-crop design; no standard-tread version ever went into regular production.

The Model HN

The first variation of the Model H appeared in early 1940, its only distinguishing feature being its single-front wheel. Designated the Model HN, it became a very popular tractor for cultivation, especially in narrowly spaced crops such as beans that were planted in rows of 28 inches or less. Deere's Decision 9000 of January 15, 1940, approved the production of this new model. The Serial Number Registers of Deere seem to indicate that the first Model HN was serial number 14983, which had a warehouse date of February 22, 1940, and was shipped on February 29, 1940, to the San Francisco branch. However, other Deere documents indicate that Decision 9000 was first put in effect on tractor 14874 on February 19, 1940. Regardless of exactly when HN production began, Deere manufactured approximately 1,100 of these tractors by production's end, and those tractors are still relatively easy to locate today. It is interesting to note that, according to Deere's Serial Number Registers, there were a few Model Hs that began production as HNs but were converted to regular Model Hs before they were fully produced, including the following:

Tractors Converted from Model HN to Model H
20564
20565
20572
20593
20906
20907
20908
20909
20910
21046
21047
21048
21050
21055

With most of their row-crop models, Deere introduced specialized versions in steps. For example, in the A Series the AW led to the AWH, which led to the A Hi-Crop. But with the Model H, Deere skipped the stage of simply widening the front end of the tractor, so they widened the front end and increased the crop clearance at the same time. The result: the Model HWH. Deere never produced a Model HW.

The Model HWH

Nearly one year after the appearance of the Model HN, Deere released yet another specialized version in the H Series. Deere's Decision 9800 of April 11, 1941, authorized production of the new Model HWH (H-Wide-High) and also outlined some features of the new model. According to that Decision, the HWH would be regularly equipped with 8x38-inch rear wheels (as opposed to the 32-inch wheels regularly fitted to the basic H). That feature contributed greatly in providing the high-clearance aspect of the model, giving it approximately 6 more inches of crop clearance. Additionally, the HWH employed a special adjustable wide front axle similar to the one used on the Model BWH. The HWH's front axle had a tread adjustment range of between 40 and 52 inches in 4-inch increments, though an optional front axle

with an increased tread range of 56 to 68 inches—also in 4-inch increments—was available. Approximately 125 HWHs were produced. The serial number of the first HWH has often been reported as being serial number 29982, which was built on March 6, 1941, but that tractor was actually the second HWH. The first HWH was actually serial number 28493, which was shipped on February 8, 1941, nearly one month earlier than the second HWH. In all, approximately 125 HWHs were produced, the last one—serial number 42842—being made in late January 1942. Thus, HWH production lasted nearly one full year.

The Model HNH

Deere revealed another new version of the Model H Series shortly after the introduction of the HWH, although

The derivatives of the Model H all shared the same basic paint schemes and decal placements. These tractor's wheels and hubs should all be painted John Deere yellow, and the exhaust stack should typically be painted black.

The Models HWH and HNH achieved the additional clearance Deere desired under the rear axles by simply having larger rear wheels. Indeed, 38-inch rear wheels sound huge for an H, but Deere made them standard on the HWH and HNH.

This HNH has a perfect three-point stance, and the Model H tackled small jobs on farms quite readily. The lights on this tractor helped perform chores at night; lights on these tractors should have clear lenses with black casings.

For farmers who liked (or needed) to use their tractors until "dark-thirty" (thirty minutes after sunset) and later, electric lights came in very handy. That feature and an electric starter were optional on the Model H beginning at serial number 27000 partway through the 1940 model year.

The Model H Options

Deere did not make very many items optional on the Model H, but those that were available are worth noting. The most important option that Deere eventually offered on the Model H was a live hydraulic pump. With that feature first available in the 1941 model year, the H John Deere was the second production tractor available with live hydraulics; the first was the Minneapolis-Moline (M-M) Model R, which had that option from its introduction in 1939. The H's hydraulic pump—which could be set up as either single or dual control, just as on the M-M R—operated via power from the governor shaft. The pump was mounted on top of the transmission case of the H, with the controls on top of the unit within easy reach of the operator.

Even though the Model H is perhaps the easiest two-cylinder Deere tractor to start by hand, Deere began to offer an electric starter on these tractors at serial number 27000, midway through 1941 model year production. At the same time, electric lights were added to the H's options list.

An often-overlooked option on the Model H was factory fenders. Quite unlike the fenders available on the Models A and B at this time, the H's fenders were more clamshell-like

Deere's optional hydraulic lift for the Model H added further to the versatility of this unit. This "live" hydraulic system—one of the earliest—received its power via the engine governor shaft. Deere offered both single- and dual-control systems with single or dual cylinders, respectively.

On the Model H, the external parts of this hydraulic unit should all be painted John Deere green with the exception of the tag as seen in this photo.

the new model was even more closely related to the HN than was the HWH. Like the HN, this model featured a single-front wheel, but it also benefited from the high-clearance aspect of the HWH. Approval for HNH production was provided through Deere's Decision 9915 of May 27, 1941, which predicted that only around 25 such units would be produced per year. The HNH used the same 38-inch rear wheels as the HWH, meaning that this model also had 6 more inches of crop clearance than did the basic H and HN. The first HNH was serial number 30172; the last was 42726. By the end of production, only 37 HNHs left the factory, making them highly desirable to collectors today.

The Special Hs with Experimental Rear Axles

The Serial Number Registers for the Model H at Deere Archives indicate that at least two 1941 model Hs were fitted with special experimental flanged rear axles, whereas the typical H featured splined rear axles. These two tractors were serial numbers 22816 and 26545, the latter also being distinguished by a special narrow rear-wheel tread.

in design. In all actuality, they more closely resembled the clamshell fenders that were later available on the Models A, B, and those that came standard on the Model R, a tractor that wouldn't appear until the 1949 model year.

Other options for the Model H included front- and rear-wheel weights and radiator shutters.

The Model H Production Lulls

As a result of material shortages caused by World War II, the Model H production experienced two major lulls. The first started immediately after H44753 was produced on April 29, 1942, and ended when the next serial-numbered H was made exactly one year later, on April 29, 1943. Only six months after that, Deere again stopped production of the H, lasting yet another year, extending from October 1943 to October 1944. The Model H number 47779 holds the latest warehouse date for a Model H before this lull: October 4, 1943. However, the last serial-numbered H produced before the lull was 47795. Production began again with serial number 47796, even though 47797 shows the earliest warehouse date: October 6, 1944.

The last Model H was produced in February 1947, bearing serial number 61116. The Model H, along with the Models L and LA, was replaced by the Model M Series—tractors that Deere would produce in its Dubuque, Iowa, factory the very next month.

The H's small size and light weight make this model very popular with collectors of all walks of life. This model is ideal for any collection, including that of city dwellers who can only store one or two tractors in their garage.

The Model M Series

In 1937, John Deere introduced its Model L. In 1939, John Deere introduced its Model H. Both were one-plow tractors. The L was more of utility garden-tractor–type unit. The H was more of a general-purpose row-crop unit. The L represented a change in thinking for Deere, possessing an upright two-cylinder engine instead of the conventional horizontal two-cylinder engine. The H also represented a change in thinking for Deere, being engineered to run off the camshaft instead of the crankshaft and being the first tractor in Deere's line available with live hydraulics.

In 1939, while a tremendous war raged in Europe, an entirely different sort of war broke out in the United States among the various tractor manufacturers; that war, too, would last until at least 1947. There were three fronts to that stateside war, and each one of them relates in some way to the Model M, a tractor that would appear after the close of the war in Europe.

The first front of the war among the U.S. tractor producers was the battle of style. It was a battle that began way back in 1935 when the Oliver Corporation introduced the Oliver-Hart Parr Model 70. It featured a slender, sleek frame, a nice-looking grille, a smooth, slender hood, louvered engine side covers, and even a hood ornament. The Oliver Hart-Parr Model 70 was the first bombshell in the war of style, and the Minneapolis-Moline Power Implement Company (M-M) made a stout return blow with its Model Z late in 1936. The Z started Visionlined styling for M-M, and the tractors jumped onto the scene with bold styling and even bolder colors: Prairie Gold with red trim. M-M continued its styling assault by launching the Models U, G, and R in the following three years, right up to the start of the 1939 model year.

In 1937, Deere stuck one foot into the styling war, almost by accident. The orchard-curved lines of its Model AOS were likely intended more for ideal orchard protection

Opposite: The Model MT better filled the void that was left in Deere's line with the discontinuation of the Model H, a tractor that had been available only in row-crop derivatives, than did the basic Model M.

The nose of the Model M doesn't look too much different from those of Deere's general-purpose, letter-series, row-crop tractors. But, get beyond the initial appearance of the sheet metal and you see an all-new sort of tractor: a true utility tractor.

and not so much for styling, but the tractor was definitely styled in its own right. Allis-Chalmers also streamlined its Model WC in the 1938 model year. Then, in 1939, the heavy-weights officially entered the war, as Deere and International unveiled their newly styled tractor lines. The eventual Model M John Deere of 1947 would be a beneficiary of the battle over style, as it continued to evolve for years to come.

The second front in the war of the U.S. tractor manu-facturers was the battle of hydraulics. A variety of companies, including Deere, had had simple hydraulic systems for a few years. However, in 1939, the battle intensified exponentially. At the beginning of that year, M-M introduced its Model R, a tractor that offered single- and dual-control live hydraulics as an option. In the summer of 1939, the new Ford-Ferguson Model 9N introduced a combined hydraulic system with three-point hitch. With the concepts introduced by those two models combined together, much experimentation

exploded in the tractor-development scene. Deere would make great strides in improving its hydraulic systems, and in 1947 the Model M was one of the earliest recipients of years of research and development.

The third front in the war of the U.S. tractor producers was the battle of small-tractor design. Both the John Deere Models L and H were produced in part to try to tap the small-farm market and get small tractors in the hands of those farmers who felt the larger tractors were either too powerful or too pricey for their operations. Not surprisingly, Deere's competitors were making strategic moves to put their tractors in the hands of those same farmers, as well. The com-petition, however, tried to do so by producing tractors that were of what is now referred to as a utility design. (Utility tractors could be used for almost anything, falling somewhere in between the design of the row-crop and standard-tread tractors. Those kinds of tractors could do almost any small

The Model M received its power from an in-line, upright, two-cylinder engine, much like that used in the Model L. only bigger.

job and many of the bigger ones; their small, compact size and sensitive steering made them handy in tight quarters, as well. Today, most "utility" tractors find their chief employment in pulling mowers and cultivating fields.) Had Deere not moved into position as quickly as it had and been so on the front lines of small-tractor production, the company might have designed a tractor more of the utility-type design that turned out to be popular with many farmers. But Deere possibly got into the battle a bit early, and in so doing had to face the consequences and devise a countermove.

Deere was possibly the earliest company to try to achieve the ideal small-tractor design, introducing its Model 62 (which would become the L the next year) in 1937. But another manufacturer came out with a small tractor in that same year: Allis-Chalmers. That model was the Allis-Chalmers Model B, and it was one of the earliest tractors to use a row-crop utility-type tractor design.

Ford-Ferguson introduced its N Series tractors in 1939 with its Model 9N. Using the Ford-Ferguson three-point hydraulic system and being adaptable to a variety of jobs, the 9N caught the attention of many farm-equipment companies. Those advantages, as well as the price of the unit, also caught the attention of many farmers.

Two other major utility-type tractors appeared on the market in 1939 courtesy of International Harvester Corporation. They were the Farmall Models A and B. The A best fit the utility tractor definition, whereas the B was more of a basic row-crop derivative, even though it was very well suited for a variety of jobs usually done by utility tractors.

By 1939, Deere had already introduced tractors that filled basically all of its line's big horsepower gaps with tractors ranging in size, horsepower, and design from the L and H to the D and G. Thus, it was not feasible for the company to think about introducing yet another tractor just to be able

To fulfill the role of a utility tractor well, the Model M featured a unique hydraulic lift system that Deere dubbed the Touch-O-Matic.

CULTIVATING SOYBEANS
JULY 1944   EXPERIMENTAL FARM
MOLINE ILL
OPERATOR   HAROLD THORNGREEN
NOTE CULTIVATOR ATTACHMENTS
AND HYDRAULIC LEVER

This experimental tractor looks very similar to the production Model M. The most interesting aspect of this tractor, however, is the location of a "JOHN DEERE" upright stencil on the nose of the tractor. *Deere & Company Archives*

to compete directly with the N Series Ford or the Farmall Models A and B. Deere decided to see how the H and L would continue to fare against the utility-type tractors of Allis-Chalmers, Ford, and International.

As World War II continued to rage in Europe, the United States tried to remain neutral. However, with the Japanese bombing of Pearl Harbor on Sunday, December 7, 1941, the United States had no choice but to enter the war officially. With that entry into World War II came a host of national regulations on production that would ultimately slow down the developmental progress of the U.S. tractor manufacturers. Despite the significantly reduced tractor production numbers and the scarceness of some materials, Deere (as well as other manufacturers) decided it was still of utmost importance to continue experimenting with new ideas. Those that did so would ultimately reap many rewards at the close of World War II.

Early in 1944, when the United States was starting to make big advances in the war in Europe, Deere &

Company produced one experimental model—the Model 69—in hopes of eventually releasing one production model that would give the company the upper hand in the quest for a feasible small-tractor design. The Model 69 bore a close resemblance to Deere's Model L, which in all actuality had a design much like Deere's competitors' row-crop utility tractors. The L, however, was much smaller than Deere's competitors' row-crop utility tractors had been, and the 69 was thus quite a bit bigger than the L in order to be more competitive.

The experimental Model 69 wasn't just a bigger version of the Model L, however. Indeed, the most noticeable difference between the two was that the 69 featured a hood design that was much more like the other row-crop tractors in Deere's line than the L. Whereas the L's hood curved down immediately behind the engine, the 69's hood extended straight back, enclosing its much larger fuel tank (which was behind the engine). Below the back section of the straight hood were side panels covering the battery of the tractor, which was located directly below the fuel tank (as opposed to being on the side of the tractor as on the L).

Testing on the Model 69 continued in both the Moline, Illinois, area and near Laredo, Texas. At least three such units were in operation by 1945, and 20 additional Model 69s were approved for production that spring. Those units quickly became known as the Model XMs (each one being followed by a number indicating its sequence in production), and Deere recognized that the model could be altered into numerous variations with ease. Deere even considered having this new model be put on tracks in order to replace the Model BO and BR Lindeman crawlers. Thus, the company sent XM-17 to the Lindeman Power Equipment Company in Yakima, Washington, to see if the unit could be successfully equipped with track assemblies. Lindeman was very successful in putting tracks on the unit, so Deere then decided to purchase Lindeman. Thus, the facilities in Yakima became known as Deere's Yakima Works, and that is where

the track assemblies would be added on the eventual production Model MC crawlers.

The Model M Production

Deere started regular production of its Model M with serial number 10001 in March 1947 at its newly constructed plant in Dubuque, Iowa. Like its experimental predecessor, the Model M was powered by an upright, in-line, two-cylinder, L-head engine. A "square" engine with its bore and stroke both being 4 inches, the M's powerplant provided about 101 cubic inches of displacement and was rated at 1,650 rpm. At the University of Nebraska Tractor Tests, the M produced 14.65 drawbar horsepower and 18.23 brake horsepower under rated load. The M also produced as much as 19.49 brake horsepower in the maximum load tests.

The Model M was the first tractor to make use of Deere's new Touch-O-Matic hydraulic system. Not exactly a

The Model M's design is closely related to that of the L, and indeed the early experimental units that led to the M very closely resembled the Model L, especially from the rear.

The M also used some features similar to those seen on the Model H. For instance, a hood much like that used on the Model H covered the engine of the new Model M. In addition, the Model M incorporated the frameless chassis design much like that seen on the popular, long-produced Model D.

So, if you take the basic chassis design of the Model L, scale it up a little, and throw in some features of the Model H such as the full-length hood, you pretty well come out with the Model M.

three-point system (since patents were still pending on the Ferguson system), the Touch-O-Matic was a very effective, very popular system. It allowed for specific depth control via the rockshaft, much like the Powr-Trol system that Deere introduced on its Waterloo-built row-crops that same year (1947). What's more, the M and its Touch-O-Matic had been designed so that attaching mounted implements would be quick and easy. Specific implements were designed for use with the system, and many of them required the operator to insert only a few pins or bolts to fully attach the unit to a tractor's lift system.

The Model MT

Since the utility design of the M did not totally satisfy all of Deere's customers (such as those that had been very sat-

isfied with the design of the Model H, for example), Deere decided to offer the Model M in a tricycle-type variation. The new tractor, the Model MT, was essentially the same tractor as the basic M; only the front axle was different. What's more, customers had a variety of front-end options on the MT. The basic narrow-set dual-wheel front end was available, as was an N-type single-front wheel and a wide-adjustable row-crop W-type front end. The MT was also available with a new dual Touch-O-Matic system. Using a split rockshaft, implements on either the front or back or left and right sides of the tractor could be controlled independently. Deere started production of the Model MT in the 1949 model year, and this version used its own serial-number run that also started with number 10001. MT production lasted into the 1952 model year, ending at serial number 40472.

Deere's Model MT more closely resembled the Model H than it did any other previous John Deere tractor. The "T" in the MT's designation denoted its tricycle front end.

The Model MC

Since Deere had purchased the Lindeman Power Equipment Company of Yakima, Washington, thereby establishing Deere's Yakima Works, production of the Model MC crawler took place in two different segments. The basic Model Ms were built at Dubuque, and then were shipped without wheels to Yakima. There, the track assemblies (which Deere had also bought the rights to) were installed on the units, and the Model MCs were born. Like the MT, these units also began production in the 1949 model year, and they also used their own serial-number run, which also started at number 10001. MC production lasted for four model years, ending with serial number 20509 in 1952.

The Model MC crawler rolled off the line as the first crawler tractor produced entirely by Deere personnel. Deere used the basic track designs as devised by the previous Lindeman Power Equipment Company (a company that Deere purchased) for this model.

The Model MI had a shorter overall height than any other wheeled M Series tractor. This was made possible by rotating the drop housings of the axles forward 90 degrees, 1thus making them essentially "push forward" housings.

The Model MI

How do you make a John Deere Model M—a tractor that has final drive drop boxes that provide an additional 8 inches of crop clearance—8 inches shorter and have an 8-inch-shorter wheelbase? Simple: rotate the basic Model M drop boxes forward one-quarter turn. That's exactly what Deere & Company did to make the John Deere Model MI. The front end of the tractor was lowered 8 inches, as well, so that the top of the hood would be level as it was on the Model M. This was accomplished by replacing the row-crop–type front axle of the M with a solid fixed-tread front axle with very short spindles. The MIs were painted industrial yellow as a regular practice, though other colors could be requested. The MI production only lasted three years, extending from the 1950 to 1952 model years. Like all of the other M Series versions, the MI used its own serial-number series, a run that started with number 10001 and ended with number 11032.

The successful M Series production terminated at the end of the 1952 model year. The series would be replaced the next year by the similar 40 Series.

Above: The Model MI, along with all of the other M Series tractors, featured a padded seat with backrest—a feature that undoubtedly made operation of these tractors more comfortable than would have been the case with a steel pan seat.

Left: Industrial yellow served as the main color for the Model MI, but other colors were available upon request. The majority of these tractors featured black lettering.

Chapter Nine

The Model R and the
End of the Letter Series

Since the introduction of the Model D in 1923, Deere hadn't actively sought after a new tractor designed specifically as a standard-tread tractor. The D was very reliable and very successful, and its production run was impressive in retrospect. However, as early as the beginning of the 1940s, Deere felt as if it had expanded the power of the D to its highest level. The company felt they needed a standard-tread tractor—or at least would eventually need one—that was bigger and more powerful than the venerable D.

Ultimately, Deere & Company decided that their new standard-tread tractor should be powered by diesel fuel, which was still relatively new in the world of tractors. Deere had been toying with the idea of diesel-powered engines for quite some time, dating back as far as 1935. It is believed that two Ds were converted to diesel on an experimental basis in the 1938 model year. By the summer of 1939, Deere had decided to expand the testing and start developing an entirely new diesel-fueled tractor model.

The new experimental units were dubbed the Model MXs. The first was built in June 1939, but it wouldn't be until 1941 that eight more were constructed. These earliest MXs had styling that was unlike anything Deere had in production at the time. Indeed, the MXs more closely resembled the Massey-Harris Model 55 than just about anything else. Deere made gradual improvements on these tractors, deciding to produce five more experimental units in 1944. By 1947, Deere had decided to build eight more MXs, tractors that by this time looked very similar to what would eventually be the Model R.

Opposite: The Model R turned over ground with ease, and, as a result, it turned many heads. It topped Deere's line horsepower-wise, overpowering both the Models D and G by a fairly respectable margin.

These two Model MX tractors are ready to take to the field for further testing. Note that these tractors are fitted with steel wheels, a feature that was actually an option on the Model R. Steel wheels came in handy, especially in rice country.
Deere & Company Archives

The Model R Unleashed

The "MX" or "diesel" project culminated in 1949 when the Model R was officially unleashed. This diesel-powered giant had an engine with a respectable displacement of 416 cubic inches, made possible by a 5-3/4x8-inch bore and stroke. It is interesting to note that, even though that was indeed a large engine, its displacement was actually smaller than that of the Model D at that time. The D featured a 501-cubic-inch engine with a bigger bore of 6-3/4 inches, but a 1-inch-shorter stroke than the R. The R's rated engine speed of 1,000 rpm was also 100 revolutions per minute faster than that of the D.

The longer stroke of the R's engine, coupled with the faster rated speed and diesel-burning aspect, meant that the

R could pack quite a punch. Under rated load, the R pounded out 43.52 belt horsepower and 34.45 drawbar horsepower. Compare that with the rated output of the D from the tests performed on it in 1940: 38.15 belt horsepower and 30.77 drawbar horsepower. Even though the differences in horsepower aren't staggering, keep in mind that the R was producing more power with 85 fewer cubic inches of displacement than the D.

Not only did the Model R prove itself to be powerful at the Nebraska Tractor Tests; it also proved itself to be very fuel-efficient. Indeed, the R—represented by tractor number 1358—set an impressive diesel fuel economy record of 17.35 horsepower hours per gallon when operating at a

maximum load brake horsepower of 48.58 horsepower. The R also proved even more efficient when operating at rated load, giving 17.63 horsepower hours per gallon in those tests. It would take five more years—and another John Deere tractor, the Model 70—to break the R's record. One year after the 70 set its record, the Model 80—the R's replacement—set the next diesel fuel economy record. Then, the next year, the John Deere 70's replacement—the Model 720—would break that record. It is obvious that Deere's first diesel-powered tractor was well engineered, and Deere certainly hasn't forgotten how to build fuel-efficient diesel engines since then, either.

Since the Model R's diesel engine had a high 16:1 compression ratio, it needed a pony motor to get started. Thus, the engine of the R was fitted with an opposed two-cylinder starting motor with a 2-3/5x2-5/16-inch bore and stroke that provided about 23 cubic inches of displacement. The pony motor spun at a very high rate of speed—4,000 rpm—and produced about 10 horsepower, which was sufficient in almost all cases to start the tractor's powerful diesel engine.

The transmission of the Model R was a five-speed unit. The speeds provided were 2-1/8, 3-1/3, 4-1/4, 5-1/3, and a comparatively fast 11-1/2 miles per hour in road gear. One reverse speed of 2-1/2 miles per hours was also provided.

Deere's Model R certainly had enough heart and mass to be able to pack a powerful punch via either the belt or the drawbar. Tipping the scales at around 7,400 pounds, the R weighed enough that it could hold its traction in delivering over 45 horsepower to the ground. In conditions where the R didn't have enough weight, wheel weights usually made up for the difference.

When viewed from a distance, the Model R is sometimes confused with the Model AR. However, up close, there is no confusion; the R's size alone takes away any doubt as to what model it is.

The Model R Options

The Model R was pretty much intended as a workhorse for doing heavy jobs, so it's not surprising that the options list for this model is among the shortest for the letter-series John Deeres. Not only was the R Deere's first production diesel tractor, it was also the first tractor Deere produced with an available live PTO. Additionally, the R was only the second Deere tractor to be available with live hydraulics, the much smaller Model H being the first. The hydraulics system on the R, however, required that the PTO be in operation to work. Thus, if you wanted live hydraulics, you had to pay the price for the PTO whether you wanted it or not. Finally, the other notable option—though

certainly not a mechanical marvel—that was a first for Deere was an enclosed steel cab.

Wheel and tire equipment for the Model R was extensive. The standard tires for this model were 14x34-inch rears mounted on 12-inch rims and 7.50x13-inch fronts. Deere made 14-inch rims optional for use with the 14x34-inch tires, as well. Larger 15x34-inch and wider 18x26-inch tires were also available in two different tread styles: regular or rice and cane type. The tractors fitted with the 15x34-inch rice and cane rear tires were fitted with 7.50x18-inch single-rib front tires as standard practice.

Most of the tractors fitted with rice and cane tires were also fitted with special mud shields for the rear axles and

brakes. These tractors are sometimes called R Rice Specials, and there were even some Rice Specials that featured factory steel wheels on both front and rear. The steel-wheeled tractors could not be shifted into fifth gear, though, as it was blocked for safety reasons. Other options for the R included wheel weights, an hour meter, and a radiator shutter.

The End of the Letter Series

The Model R was the last of the letter-series John Deere tractors in production. The last R—serial number 22293—rolled off the assembly line on September 17, 1954. Shipments of the Model R would continue as late as January 1955. But for Deere, the 1954 model marked the end of the letter-series tractors era, and the R was the last model to both start and end production in that era. The R was also the biggest and most powerful tractor of its era, as well. The Model R diesel was truly the ultimate letter-series John Deere two-cylinder tractor.

But the end of the letter-series tractors was not only an ending; it was also a beginning. For Deere & Company, the letter series had begun the company's tractor production, that is, if you include the Waterloo Boy Models R and N. The

letter-series tractors had launched John Deere into the tractor industry, and the tractors proved themselves very reliable. Along with that, customers began to associate high quality with the John Deere brand, a feeling that spread to almost all of Deere's products over time.

The letter-series tractors set many records in their time, some of which stand to this day. For the entire tractor industry, the Model D holds the record for the longest production run, lasting over 30 years, from 1923 to 1953. If one considers the Model D as the first tractor in the letter series (excluding the Waterloo Boy models), then it was in production for all but one of the years of John Deere letter-series tractor production. The Model B set the John Deere sales record, with over 300,000 units finding their way onto the farms of the world and into the hearts of their owners. The Model A followed close behind in sales, with just under 300,000 units produced.

The two-cylinder era of John Deere began with the Waterloo Boy Models N and R, plus John Deere's D. The rest of its letter-series tractors carried that torch for 32 additional years. Even though the end of the letter series did not mean the end of Deere's two-cylinder era, it certainly had made up the bulk of it.

For many collectors, the Model R's weight alone takes it out of their consideration, as many collectors don't have a trailer that's stout enough to handle toting the R. However, tractor pullers love this model, even though its great grandchild, the Model 830, is even more popular with those enthusiasts.

Appendix

Serial Numbers

In this appendix, the serial-number ranges for all of the letter-series John Deere tractors are given. When large blocks of serial numbers were either scrapped or not used, these blocks of numbers are so indicated. Numerous other individual tractors were scrapped throughout the production of these models, but it is not feasible to list every serial number of every tractor that was scrapped. Thus, an asterisk (*) is located next to blocks of serial numbers in which certain individual tractors are known to be scrapped. This serial-number listing is as complete and accurate as possible.

The Waterloo Boy Model R

1915	1026 to 1400
1916	1401 to 3555
1917	3556 to 6981
1918	6982 to 9055
1919	9056 to unknown

The Waterloo Boy Model N

1917	10020
1918	10221 to 13460
1919	13461 to 18923
1920	18924 to 27025
1921	27026 to 27811
1922	27812 to 28118
1923	28119 to 29519
1924	29520 to unknown

The Model A row-crops (unstyled)

1934	410000 to 412868
1935	412869 to 424024
1936	424025 to 442150
1937	442151 to 466786
1938	466787 to 476221
	(476222 to 476999 scrapped)

The Model A row-crops (early styled)

1939	477000 to 478115
	(478116 to 478199 scrapped)
	478200 to 478472
	(478473 to 478499 scrapped)
	478500 to 487249
	(487250 to 487360 scrapped)
1940	488000 to 498535
	(498536 to 498558 scrapped)
	498559 (498560 to 498999 scrapped)
1941	499000 to 510238
1942	510239 to 520003
1943	520004 to 522349
	(522350 to 522599 scrapped)
	522600 to 524422
1944	524423 to 532936
	(532937 to 532999 scrapped)
	533000 to 536541
	(536542 to 536999 scrapped)
	537000 to 542626
	(542627 to 542699 scrapped)
1945	542700 to 555333
1946	555334 to 569609
1947	569610 to 583326
	(583327 to 583999 scrapped)

The Model A row-crops (late styled)

1947	584000 to 587348
1948	587349 to 611920
1949	611921 to 628499
	(628500 to 628536 scrapped)
	628537 to 640245
1950	640246 to 647069
	(647070 to 647999 scrapped)
	648000 to 666306
1951	666307 to 676746
	(676747 to 676799 scrapped)
	676800 to 677949
	(677950 to 677999 scrapped)
	678000 to 682601
1952	682602 to 684380
	(684381 scrapped)
	684382 to 684484 (684485 scrapped)
	684486 to 685052 (685053 scrapped)
	685054 to 700140
	(700141 to 700199 scrapped)
	700200 to 703384
	(703385 to 703999 scrapped)

The Models AR, AO

Year	Serial numbers
1936	250000 to 253520
1937	253521 to 255415
1938	255416 to 256699
1939	256700 to 257989
	(257990 to 257999 scrapped)
1940	258000 to 258467
	(258468 to 258799 scrapped)
	258800 to 259335
	(259336 to 259999 scrapped)
1941	260000 to 261124
1942	261125 to 262156
1943	262157 to 262497
	(262498 to 262699 scrapped)
1944	262700 to 264199
	(264200 to 264299 scrapped)
1945	264300 to 265534
1946	265535 to 266642
1947	266643 to 268409
1948	268410 to 270679
1949	270680 to 272984
1950	272985 to 276076
1951	276077 to 278698
1952	278699 to 282349
1953	282350 to 284074

The Model AO-S

Year	Serial numbers
1937	1000 to 1497
	(1498 to 1525 scrapped)
	1526 to 1538
1938	1539 to 1693
	(1694 to 1696 scrapped)
	1697 to 1699
1939	1700 to 1771
	(1772 to 1799 scrapped)
1940	1800 to 1836
	(1837 to 1849 scrapped)
	1850 to 1891 (1892 to 2999 scrapped)

The Model B row-crops (unstyled)

Year	Serial numbers
1934	1000 to 1082
1935	1083 to 12011*
1936	12012 to 27388*
1937	27389 to 49301*
1938	49302 to 58246*
	(58247 to 59999 scrapped)

The Model B row-crops (early styled)

Year	Serial numbers
1939	60000 to 78525*
1940	78526 to 95201*
	(95202 to 95999 scrapped)
1941	96000 to 118720*
1942	118721 to 136314*
1943	136315 to 149218*
1944	149219 to 166879*
1945	166880 to 179787*
1946	179788 to 190677*
1947	190678 to 200247*
	(200248 to 200999 scrapped)

The Model B row-crops (late styled)

Year	Serial numbers
1947	201000 to 209294*
1948	209295 to 230043*
1949	230044 to 253024*
1950	253025 to 275241*
1951	275242 to 293029*
1952	293030 to 310772*

The Models BR, BO

Year	Serial numbers
1936	325000 to 326654
1937	326655 to 328071*
	(328072 to 328099 scrapped)
1938	328100 to 328890
	(328891 to 328999 scrapped)
1939	329000 to 330212
1940	330213 to 330539
	(330540 to 330549 scrapped)
	330550 to 331144
	(331145 to 331499 scrapped)
	331500 to 332038
1941	332039 to 332426*
1942	332427 to 332779
1943	332780 to 333155
1944	333156 to 333523
	(333524 to 333599 scrapped)
1945	333600 to 335640*
1946	335641 to 336745*
1947	336746 to 337514
	(337515 to 337999 scrapped)

The Model D Series (unstyled)

Year	Serial numbers
1923	30401 to 30450
1924	30451 to 31303
1925	31304 to 31320 (31321 to 31412 used for the 1924 model Waterloo Boy Model Ns)
	31413 to 35308
1926	35309 to 43409
1927	43410 to 54553
1928	54554 to 60256
1929	60257 to 95366*
1930	95367 to 103487*
	(103488 to 103515 scrapped)
	103516 (103517 to 103520 scrapped)
	103521 to 103523
	(103524 scrapped)
	103525 to 103526
	(103527 to 103528 scrapped)
	103529 to 103533
	(103534 to 103542 scrapped)
	103543 to 103545
	(103546 scrapped)
	103547 to 103550
	(103551 to 103552 scrapped)
	103553 (103554 to 103558 scrapped)
	103559 (103560 to 103607 scrapped)
	103608 to 109943*
1931	109944 to 115508*
1932	115509 to 115664*
1933	115665 to 116085
	(116086 to 116093 cancelled)
	116094 to 116112
	(116113 cancelled)
	116114 to 116125
	(116126 to 116138 cancelled)
	116139 to 116142
	(116143 to 116162 cancelled)
	116163 to 116272
1934	116273 to 119080*
	(119081 to 119099 scrapped)
1935	119100 to 125078*
1936	125079 to 130651*
	(130652 scrapped)
1937	130653
	(130654 to 130699 scrapped)
	130700 to 136725*
	(136726 to 136799 scrapped)

136800 to 137993*
    (137994 to 138003 scrapped)
138004 to 138412*
1938 138413 to 142287*
    (142288 to 142299 scrapped)
1939 142300 to 143568*
    (143569 to 143799 scrapped)

The Model D Series (styled)

1939	143800 to 146325*
	(146326 to 146499 scrapped)
1940	146500 to 148871*
1941	148872 to 151886*
1942	151887 to 154469*
1943	154470 to 155028*
1944	155029 to 158453*
1945	158454 to 158501
	(158502 to 158599 scrapped)
	158600 to 161374*
	(161375 to 161399 scrapped)
	161400 to 161700
1946	161701 to 164896*
1947	164897 to 171954*
1948	171955 to 180811*
1949	180812 to 187701*
	(187702 scrapped)
1950	187703 (187704 scrapped)
	187705 to 189368*
	(189369 to 189400 scrapped)
	189401 to 189578
	(189579 to 189599 scrapped)
1951	189600 to 190960*
1952	190961 to 191178
	(191179 to 191199 scrapped)
	191200 to 191404
1953	191405 to 191670

The Model G (unstyled)

1937	1000 to 2149*
	(2150 to 2199 scrapped)
	2200 to 2599*
1938	2600 to 7000*
	(7001 to 7099 scrapped)
1939	7100 to 8899
	(8900 to 9199 scrapped)
1940	9200 to 10140*
1941	10141 to 11560*
1942	11561 to 12192*
	(12193 to 12999 scrapped)

The Model GM

1942	13000 to 13457*
1943	13458 to 13747
1945	13748 to 14507*
	(14508 to 14599 scrapped)
	14600 to 15779*
1946	15780 to 18487*
	(18488 to 18699 scrapped)
	18700 to 18852
1947	18853 to 22112*
	(22113 to 22999 scrapped)

The Model G Series (early styled)

1947	23000 to 25234
1948	25235 to 25671
	(25672 to 25999 scrapped)

The Model G Series (late styled)

1948	26000 to 32456
1949	32457 to 39160*
1950	39161 to 46808*
1951	46809 to 53478*
1952	53479 to 60667*
	(60668 to 60675 scrapped)
	60676 to 60680
	(60681 to 60699 scrapped)
	60700 to 63137*
1953	63138 to 64530

The Model C

1928	200111 to 200202*
	(200203 to 200210 not used)

The Model GP (Standard)

1928	200211 to 202565
1929	202566 to 216138
1930	216139 to 224056*
	(224057 to 224099 scrapped)
	224100 to 224320*
1931	224321 to 228665*
1932	228666 to 229050
1933	229051 to 229215*
1934	229216 to 229487
	(229488 to 229500 scrapped)
	229501 to 230368*
	(230369 to 230399 scrapped)
	230400 to 230514
1935	230515 to 230745

The Model GPWT

1929	400000 to 400935
1930	400936 to 402740
1931	402741 to 404769
1932	404770 to 405109
1933	405110 to unknown

The Model H Series

1939	1000 to 1001* (1002 scrapped)
	1003 to 1004
	(1005 to 1012 scrapped)
	1013 (1014 to 1015 scrapped)
	1016 (1017 to 1043 scrapped)
	1044 (1045 to 1103 scrapped)
	1104 to 9910*
	(9911 to 9999 scrapped)
1940	10000 to 21143*
	(21144 to 21499 scrapped)
	21500 to 26735*
	(26736 to 26999 scrapped)
	27000 to 35698*
1941	35699 to 44753*
1942	44754 to 45641*
1943	45642 to 47795*
1945	47796 to 50293*
	(50294 to 50499 scrapped)
	50500 to 53326*
1946	53327 to 56087*
	(56088 to 56399 scrapped)
	56400 to 58613*
1947	58614 to 61116*
	(61117 to 61999 scrapped)

The Model 62

1937	621000 to 621078

The Model L (unstyled)

1938	621079 to 622580
	(622581 to 624999 scrapped)

The Model L (styled)

1939	625000 to 628499 (628500 to 628999 no info, assumed scrapped)
1940	629000 to 633079
1941	633080 to 633341
	(633342 number destroyed)
	633343 to 634841 (634842 to 639999 no info, assumed scrapped)
1942	640000 to 640737
1944	640738 to 641037
1945	641038 to 641957
1946	641958 to 642038 (642039 to 642399 no info, assumed scrapped)

The Model LA Series

1941	1001 to 1908
	(1909 number destroyed)
	1910 to 3120
1942	3121 to 6028
1944	6029 (6030 number lost)
	6031 to 8269
1945	8270 to 10387
1946	10388 to 13475 (13476 to 13600 no info, assumed scrapped)

The Model LI

1941	50001 to 50341
1942	50342 to 50766
1943	50767 to 50815
1944	50816 to 50871 (50872 number lost)
	50873 to 51017
1945	51018 to 51199 (51200 number lost)
	51201 to 51518
1946	51519 to 52019 (52020 to 52073 no info, assumed scrapped)

The Model M

1947	10001 to 13733
1948	13734 to 25603
1949	25604 to 35658
1950	35659 to 43524
1951	43525 to 50579
1952	50580 to 55799

The Model MT

1949	10001 to 14727
1950	14728 to 25272
1951	25273 to 32812
1952	32813 to 40472

The Model MC

1949	10001 to 11092
1950	11093 to 13373
1951	13374 to 15340
1952	15341 to 20509

The Model MI

1950	10001 to 10292
1951	10293 to 10684
1952	10685 to 11032

The Model R

1949	1000 to 2414*
1950	2415 to 3111ᴬ
	(3112 to 3199 scrapped)
	3200 to 6367*
1951	6368 to 7795*
	(7796 to 7899 scrapped)
	7900 to 8380*
	(8381 to 8399 scrapped)
	8400 to 9292*
1952	9293 to 15092*
1953	15093 to 19092
1954	19093 to 22293

Index